Backyard Pets

Activities for Exploring Wildlife
Close to Home

Carol A. Amato

Illustrated by Cheryl Kirk Noll

John Wiley & Sons, Inc.

This book is dedicated to my daughters, Maria and Nicole,
who taught me to see the smallest creatures through
their eyes of wonder.

My acknowledgments to the dedicated staff and volunteers at
Blue Hill Trailside Museum in Milton, Massachusetts, who bring
the joys of the natural world to so many visitors.

Published by John Wiley & Sons, Inc., New York
Published simultaneously in Canada

Design and production by Navta Associates, Inc.

The publisher and the author have made every reasonable effort to ensure that the
experiments and activities in the book are safe when conducted as instructed, but they
assume no responsibility for any damage caused or sustained while performing them.
Parents, guardians, and teachers should supervise young readers who undertake the
experiments and activities in this book.

ISBN 0-471-41693-2

Printed in the United States of America

10   9   8   7   6   5   4   3   2   1

Contents

Introduction

Are you really interested in the world around you? Are you curious about why animals do some of the things they do? When you see a toad or a frog or even one of those roly-poly pill bugs, do you want to bring it home and take care of it? If you answered yes to most of these questions, then this book is definitely for you! Don't worry if you don't live near forests or ponds. You can find all sorts of critters right in your own backyard, and even between the cracks of city sidewalks.

I'll be honest right from the start. In the special world of critter caretaking, there are lots of rules. But if you're careful to follow these rules, your experience will be more rewarding, and your backyard pets will thank you! You must remember above all that living things, regardless of how small they are, deserve our respect and good care. Each small critter is an important player in the **biodiversity** of its surroundings. This means that every living thing (including ourselves) is dependent for survival on a network that links all of us together.

The more you know about your temporary pets, the more likely you are to care for them well. That's why most of the questions in this book are based on an animal's needs for survival, such as:

Habitat—Where does the animal live?

Food and water—What does the animal eat and drink?

Adaptations for protection—How does the animal survive in its environment and avoid predators?

Locomotion—How does the animal move around?

Reproduction—How does the animal have babies and take care of them?

Communication—How does the animal send messages to others?

Most of the critters we will discuss can be kept comfortably for a short period of time while you observe them. You may be able to keep some of them longer with diligent care, but if you are the forgetful type, don't consider it. Even with the best of care, you know that the animal would much prefer to be roaming around in its habitat . . . free. In some chapters, we will just observe small critters in the wild—the open environment where they belong.

Once you've brought your critter home and made it comfortable, you will be ready to do some investigating to find out more about it. The suggestions in this book serve only as a guide. You may want to learn more about your critter on your own.

Scientists have divided up the millions of known animals into 26 groups. These groups are called **phyla**. Each phylum is a broad collection of animals that have important characteristics in common but may be quite different in others. Phyla are divided into **classes,** classes into **orders,** orders into **families,** and families into **genera.** Each genus is made up of different **species.** The animals that are most closely related are grouped together within these categories. You may want to do some research about the classification of the creatures described in this book.

The investigations in this book are modeled on what scientists do when they want to learn about something new. They may start with a hunch, a question, or an idea. They then gather information about the question. They may form a **hypothesis,** or theory, about why something is the way it is, and then make a **prediction** about the outcome of an experiment based on their hypothesis. Then they do some experiments to test the hypothesis and see whether their predictions come true. Scientists record their data, or information, so that they'll have an easy way to see their results. After many **trials** (repeats of the investigation), they may even be able to make **conclusions** about what they have observed and studied.

How would you like to be a chef for your backyard birds, tame a toad, and have a land snail race? In addition to the scientific investigations, this book also provides lots of activities you can do with your backyard pet that are just for fun!

In part 2, you'll learn how to attract wildlife to your backyard. This will make it possible for you to study nature any time you choose and to practice your nature detective skills year-round. You will discover how to make a garden filled with flowers that attract many kinds of lovely butterflies and hummingbirds. You will learn how to make simple birdfeeders so that you can invite birds to your backyard habitat. And there's so much more you can learn!

To attract wildlife to your backyard, you will need to provide critters with what they need to survive: a place to live or to visit, food, water, and protection. The idea is to copy a bit of nature so that a variety of creatures will feel right at home in your backyard. You don't necessarily need a lot of space. Even if you live in the city and don't have a backyard, you can attract butterflies and birds using flower boxes and window birdfeeders.

You will not need any fancy scientific equipment to do any of the activities in this book. It would be good, however, to put together a basic "nature detective" kit so that you will be ready for any critter adventures that may just happen to come your way. Here are some suggestions:

Hand lens (magnifying glass)

Binoculars

Supply of pencils and a notebook (to record observations)

Small camera

Mesh bug-catching container (can be purchased) or a small, lidded plastic jar

You'll think of some of your own supplies as well. One of your greatest tools will be nature guidebooks about insects, birds, amphibians, flowers, trees, and so forth. There are many kinds in the library, some of them designed just for kids.

Now show your parents this book and ask them if you can keep that critter for a while!

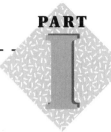
Bringing Backyard Pets Home

1 Slimy Snails and Slithery Slugs

Snail and Slug Basics

There are more than 80,000 species of slugs and snails in the world. They come in many colors and many sizes: some are as small as a dot, to the huge ones more than a foot (30 cm) long. All snails and slugs are members of a large phylum of animals, called **mollusks,** that have been on the earth for millions of years. They may live in the ocean, in freshwater, or on land, even in trees! A mollusk is a soft-bodied animal with a head, a muscular foot, and internal organs. Mussels, scallops, clams, squid, and octopuses are members of this phylum. The clam uses the foot to burrow into sand or mud. In octopuses and squids, the foot has developed into **tentacles** for grabbing prey.

The foot of the snail or slug touches the ground as the animal creeps along. All mollusks are **invertebrates,** which do not have bony skeletons. Instead, they have an outside skeleton such as a shell. Squids and octopuses and even slugs have tiny shells under their skin that help to support their bodies. Snails and slugs are classed as **gastropods,** which is Latin for "belly foot." Isn't it amazing how members of the same family of creatures have adapted in different ways to suit their individual needs for survival?

Snail

Slug

We will concentrate on land snails and slugs. You may also want to observe other kinds of gastropods. If you have lots more questions about snails and slugs, read on! The slimy fun has just begun!

Where can I find them?

Look under rocks and damp stones, leaves, flowerpots, and all kinds of vegetation, especially in gardens. Snails and slugs like moist places, so search for them after a rainfall or early in the morning on foggy days. You can become a gastropod detective by looking for them at night with a flashlight. During the day, if you examine the ground, or even the sidewalk, you may see their slime trails glistening in the sun. If the trail is moist, a snail or slug may be nearby. Remember, good detectives observe details closely.

How can I catch them?

On your search, take with you a container such as a coffee can or a plastic container. Punch holes in the top so the snails can breathe. You may be outside for a while, searching in different places, so you don't want your snails or slugs to escape or be uncomfortable. Put soil or leaves in the bottom of the container. When you find a snail, place it gently in the container. Be careful not to pull at the shell if the snail is attached to a surface; if the shell separates from the snail's body or is cracked, the snail will die. Gently slide a leaf under the snail, and it will usually lift off easily. If it doesn't, leave it alone and search elsewhere. You want to consider the critter's well-being at all times.

How can I keep them?

To set up a more permanent home for your snails, you can use a wide-mouthed glass jar, a small glass or plastic aquarium, or any transparent container. Be sure your container is clean, with no bits of dried mayonnaise or tomato sauce inside!

Put a few inches of dirt in the bottom of the container, and moisten the dirt using a spray bottle. Place a handful or two of dead leaf litter (decaying and broken leaves) on top of the dirt. Add some whole dead leaves and some small rocks and branches for the snails to climb on.

Don't overcrowd your gastropods. Snails and slugs can live together, but don't put more than two or three in a large jar, or four or five in a small plastic aquarium tank. Cover the container with a piece cut from your mom's old panty hose (with her permission!) Fasten this around the top of the jar with a rubber band. You can use plastic wrap instead, with holes punched in the top, also fastened with an elastic. Plastic wrap is good to use because it holds in more moisture. Just be careful that the holes in the plastic don't enlarge, or the snails will escape. The idea is to be sure that your snails or slugs get plenty of fresh air.

Keep the container out of direct sunlight and away from vents and radiators. You must supply your gastropods with water daily, or they will dry up and die. Mist them with a spray bottle or flick water from your fingers into the container. Keep the soil slightly damp, but don't let it get too soggy.

Clean the slime and droppings off the sides of your container each week. About once every two months (if you're still entertaining your guests), clean out the entire container and wash it in soapy water. Be careful to look for eggs before you empty the container. If you have cared for your snails well, you may find a cluster of tiny white eggs

Snail habitats: Jar or plastic container, with mister/terrarium

buried in the dirt or under rocks or leaves. *Always remember to wash your hands well after handling your snail, or any creature.*

If you've neglected to spray your snails for a few days and they seem inactive, don't panic! Just dip them briefly in water and spray the container and their food well, and they may revive.

What should I feed them?

Put fresh food in your snail or slug's home at least every other day, or whenever you see the old food looking wilted. You can experiment with a variety of foods, such as:

- ◆ lettuce (never iceberg, which has very little nutrition; romaine is best)
- ◆ spinach and other leafy greens
- ◆ mushrooms
- ◆ fruits, such as apples, strawberries, and tomatoes
- ◆ other vegetables, such as cucumber and carrots

Be inventive, but stay away from foods like pizza and hot dogs! Wash all food to remove pesticides. Since snails need calcium for their shells, give them clean (uncooked) eggshells or a piece of cuttlebone, which you can get at a pet store.

Snail and Slug Observations

Now that you have made your guests comfortable, you will want to find out more about them. First, observe your snail or slug closely with a magnifying glass. In this way, you will more easily understand the answers provided here to the questions about snails and slugs, and you may even discover some answers for yourself!

Find out More about Snails and Slugs

How do land snails and slugs protect themselves?

As you can see, when a snail is threatened, it can pull itself back into its shell. However, it also has a hard, flat plate called an **operculum,** which it can slam shut like a door if danger is near. The operculum helps to seal in moisture so that the snail can go for longer periods without water. A slug is not so fortunate. The best it can do is to try to squeeze itself as small as it can under its mantle. If it can't hide from its prey, it's pretty much a goner!

The anatomy of the snail. Look for these body parts:

Breathing hole: The opening to the snail's air sacs.

Mantle: A soft-tissue layer on top of the snail that secretes a liquid as the snail grows. The mantle is made of protein, minerals, and calcium and hardens to become the shell.

Operculum: A hard, flat plate that can slam shut like a door if danger is near.

Radula: The snail's tongue, which has tiny, sharp teeth. The snail rubs its radula against its food to scrape off small bites.

Tentacles: Four slender, flexible feelers that act as sensors. The longer pair have eye spots, and the shorter pair detect odors.

External

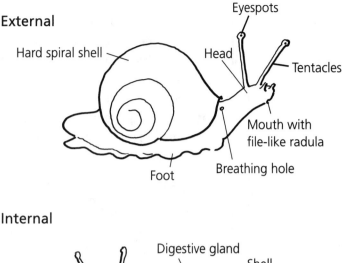

Eyespots
Hard spiral shell
Head
Tentacles
Mouth with file-like radula
Foot
Breathing hole

Internal

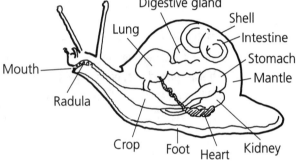

Digestive gland
Shell
Lung
Intestine
Stomach
Mantle
Mouth
Radula
Crop
Foot
Heart
Kidney

Do snails and slugs breathe?

Yes. Look for the open hole on the side of your snail or slug. That opening is the breathing hole to its lung. The lung is not like ours but has air sacs with a lot of little blood vessels in its surface area to pick up oxygen.

How does a snail or slug move?

Observe your snail or slug by placing it in a clear plastic food container or on a piece of glass. Look at it from below. Can you see the foot muscles moving in waves? The waves are muscle contractions that move from back to front to move the snail or slug forward. To move along easily and smoothly, the snail or slug releases **slime** from a mucus gland near its head. Turn the container upside down. Does the snail or slug fall off? The slime is so sticky that it acts like glue. The creature can still move by releasing the pressure along its foot. The slime also helps it to absorb moisture as it travels along, and it protects the foot from rough objects.

Can a snail or slug see or hear?

Observe your snail or slug with a magnifying glass. Do you see anything that might resemble eyes? If you look very closely, you will find two eyes that look like dots at the tips of its long upper tentacles. These eyeballs can only sense light. The snail raises its tentacles to look around. These gastropods also have light sensors on their lips, foot, and mantle. They rely more on feeling to find their way, using their short bottom tentacles.

Very gently tap one of the tentacles with the tip of your finger, barely making contact. What happens? The snail or slug can pull its tentacles back into its head when it senses danger. Don't do this frequently or you may seriously injure it!

These animals cannot hear as we do, but they use their other senses to find out about their surroundings.

How does a snail or slug eat?

Snails and slugs have scent detectors on their upper tentacles that alert them to the chemicals given off by food. They have no teeth but do have toothy tongues! The tongue has rows of tiny, sharp teeth called a **radula.** As the animal rubs its food, it scrapes off small bits.

How can you tell a boy snail or slug from a girl one?

Would you believe that each snail is both a boy *and* a girl? How can that be? They are **hermaphrodites:** each individual has the reproductive parts of both a male and a female. This is a very useful trait for animals who live solitary lives and don't meet up with their kind very often. The snail can mate with any other snail that it meets!

How long do snails and slugs live?

Usually three to four years, but a few old-timers reach seven or eight years.

Do snails and slugs have any enemies?

Snails and slugs are eaten by birds, foxes, badgers, and moles. Baby land snails are eaten by rodents when their shells are still thin. It's not like they can make a fast getaway!

Something's covering the opening of my snail's shell, and it won't come out. Is it dead?

If your snail is cold or dry, or if it hasn't had food in a while, it may seal itself shut with a dried slime. This **epiphragm** lets in air but doesn't let moisture out. Sometimes the snail can stay alive for weeks or even months like this. Try dipping your snail quickly in water and placing it on a damp lettuce leaf. If it doesn't revive in a day or so, you'll know it did not survive. Return it to the place where you found it, though, just in case!

Do snails and slugs hibernate in the winter?

In winter, snails and slugs hibernate (kind of like a long sleep) until spring. They find sheltered places like under rocks, between logs, in cracks in walls, and the like. Snails seal their operculum with an epiphragm that hardens to keep them warm and toasty. Slugs have to settle for burrowing deep into the soil and hoping for a mild winter.

Snail and Slug Investigations

Favorite Foods

Ask:

Do snails and slugs have favorite foods?

Hypothesize:

From what you know about snails, make a prediction about what kinds of food they prefer.

Procedure:

1. Place the same food in the two containers and mist lightly with a spray bottle.
2. Add 1 or 2 snails or slugs to each container.
3. Check the containers in 4 to 8 hours.

Results:

Which foods did your two sets of critters eat? Record your data on a chart like the one below:

	Snail Group 1	Snail Group 2
Cucumber		
Lettuce		
Mushroom		
Carrot		

Conclusions:

What does the data chart show about the snails or slugs? How do the two sets of critters compare with one another? Can you draw any conclusions based on your data and your observations?

Think about it:

Would you get the same results tomorrow? If you used different snails, would you get different results?

> **You will need:**
>
> 2 flat food containers
>
> plastic wrap (make air holes in the top)
>
> rubber bands large enough to fit around food containers
>
> various types of food that you select
>
> 2 to 4 snails or slugs

Dark or Light?

You will need:

a plastic container
a dark towel or cloth
a land snail or slug

Ask:

Do snails and slugs prefer dark or light places?

Hypothesize:

From what you have learned and observed about snails, make a prediction about whether they prefer darkness or light.

Procedure:

1. Put the container in a well-lit place.
2. Lay the cloth over half of the container.
3. Put the snail or slug in the center of the container.

Results:

Did the snail or slug move toward or away from the light? Repeat this procedure several times and record your results.

Conclusions:

Was your prediction correct? Can you make any inferences based on your collected results?

Think about it:

In the wild, snails prefer dark places. Do you think this preference aids in their survival?

Slime Trail

You will need:

a piece of wood
an index card
pieces of fruit or vegetable that your snail or slug likes
your guest snail or slug

Ask:

Do slugs and snails use their slime trails to find their way back to their feeding places (as some scientists believe)?

Hypothesize:

Have you observed your snails as they search for food? Based on your observations and what you know about snails, make a prediction about their ability to find their feeding places.

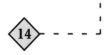

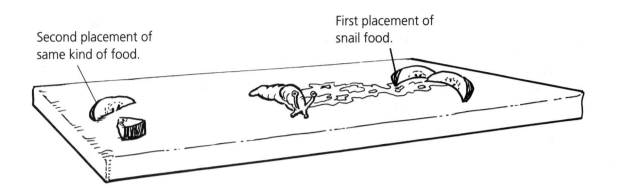

Second placement of same kind of food.

First placement of snail food.

Procedure:

1. Wet the piece of wood and let it dry naturally for about an hour.
2. Place a piece of snail food on one end of the wood piece.
3. Put the snail or slug in the middle of the wood piece.
4. Observe the snail or slug until it finds the food.
5. Put the snail back in the middle of the piece of wood. Gently slide a stiff piece of paper, such as an index card, under a slug to lift it.
6. Now place a piece of the same kind of food at the other end of the wood.

Results:

Does the snail or slug return to the food on its old slime trail, or does it go to the food in the new location?

Conclusions:

Can you draw any conclusions from this experiment? Do you need more trials? Did you get the same or different results each time you tried this?

Think about it:

Do you think the results of this experiment would be different if you put the snail or slug and the food on soil or grass? Try this activity using one or both of these. After observing the creature's trailmaking, can you predict if or how it might follow slime trails in its native habitat?

Snail and Slug Activities

Snail or Slug Races

Just how fast do you think snails or slugs can move?
Do snails move faster than slugs? Try this fun activity to find out.
No coaching or poking of gastropods allowed!

You will need:

2 or more snails or slugs (or combine both species in your race)

a foot of yarn or string

dark-colored construction or other paper

a ruler

a watch or a clock with a second hand

Procedure:

1. Set a time limit for the snail race, such as 3 to 5 minutes. (Most gastropods take a while to begin moving!)
2. Place the snails side by side at one end of the paper.
3. When the time period is up, measure the slime trails left by the snails and slugs with the yarn or string and hold the yarn up to the ruler.
4. The contestant with the longest slime trail wins!

Make a Radula

Now that you know that snails and slugs have teeth-like radulae, you may wonder how they work. Try this activity to find out, but don't try to eat your own veggies this way!

You will need:

a piece of sandpaper, at least 8 inches (25 cm) by 6 inches (15 cm)

glue

a piece of cardboard about 8 inches by 6 inches (25 by 15 cm) (cut into a tongue shape if you'd like)

Procedure:

1. Cut out small "teeth" from the sandpaper.
2. Following the diagram, glue the sandpaper teeth in a row along the edge of the piece of cardboard. This will be Row A.
3. Glue a second row of teeth partly on top of Row A to make Row B.
4. Continue making and gluing layers of sandpaper teeth.
5. Let your radula dry for several hours or overnight.
6. Now rub your radula against a piece of lettuce. Consider yourself a new species of giant snail! (Sorry, no pizza for you anymore!)

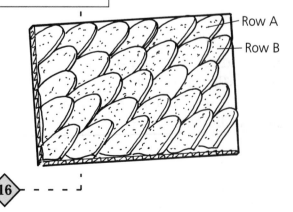

Row A

Row B

Snails for Lunch

Don't worry! Although many people just love cooked
snails (*escargots*, in French), in this activity you'll create a lunch in
honor of your favorite gastropods. You can invite all of your snail-
loving friends (and their pets). This might be especially fun as a
going-away party for your snails or slugs when you're ready to
release them!

Menu

Slug dogs: Little cocktail hot dogs (baby slugs) with toothpick tentacles. (Those with heartier appetites can try our giant slugs—
regular-size hot dogs, with carrot-stick feelers.) Served with
mustard and relish slime. Grassy sauerkraut optional.

Little logs: These are great places for snails and slugs to hide! For
you, they are French fries. (The frozen kind are quick and easy.)

Snail gourmet salad: This crispy salad has everything a snail loves:
romaine lettuce, carrots, cucumbers, mushrooms, and whatever other veggies you like. Serve with slimy vinaigrette salad
dressing (oil and vinegar), but skip the dressing for your snail
guests.

Snail sticky buns: A sweet dessert in honor
of our esteemed and soon to be
departing guests. Roll refriger-
ated packaged dough into
snail shapes and dip them
in slime—"sticky bun"
frosting. Even the
snails would lick
their fingers (or
feet!) if these were
part of their diet.

2 Terrific Toads

Toad Basics

Have you ever wondered why toads
have so many warts? Do you think you
will catch warts if you touch a toad? Do
you want to find out the differences between
a frog and a toad? Well, this is a good place to begin!

Frog

Both frogs and toads are **amphibians.** Amphibians have a
strong tie to the water, but some live mostly on land or only part of
the time in the water. The many species of toads live in all kinds of
world habitats, ranging from deserts and high mountains to tropi-
cal rainforests. It's no wonder that you might find toads in your
own backyard no matter where you live!

Frogs and toads are both **vertebrates** (animals with backbones) that begin life in the water, then move onto land. Mother
frogs and toads lay their eggs in ponds.
Then the babies hatch as tadpoles, taking
air from the water through **gills,** in the
same way that fish do. The tadpoles are
gradually transformed into air-breath-
ing creatures as they grow legs and
develop lungs. This process, called
metamorphosis, may take a few weeks or
many years, depending on the kind, or
species.

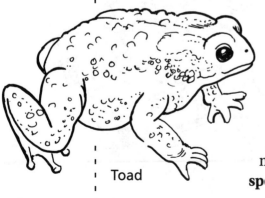

Toad

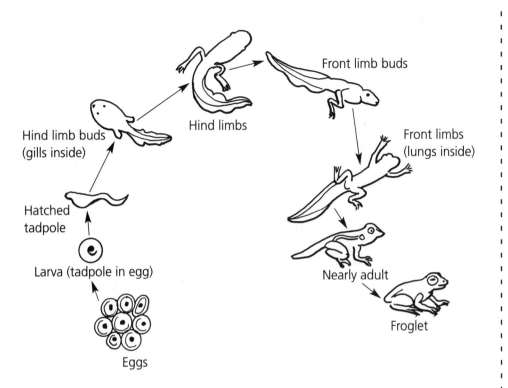

Hind limb buds
(gills inside)

Hind limbs

Front limb buds

Front limbs
(lungs inside)

Hatched
tadpole

Larva (tadpole in egg)

Nearly adult

Froglet

Eggs

In this chapter, we focus on our friends the toads. True toads belong to the family **Bufonidae.** There are more than 340 species of true toads in the world. The genus *Bufo* includes more than 70 species of toads in North America alone.

Where can I find them?

Often, as you walk through the woods or play in your yard, you just happen to see a toad by chance. If you don't want to count on chance to find a toad, try looking in gardens, fields, or forests, where toads like to burrow in the earth. They can also be found in vacant lots right in the middle of the city, especially if breeding ponds are nearby. Since toads like small, secret places, look under flowerpots, porches, and loose boards that have been lying around. Most toads are **nocturnal:** they come out at night to hunt, so you might search for them then. If you don't have much of a backyard, walk (with an adult) in the country or a wooded park at night. Bring a flashlight and shine it on the ground as you walk, since light often attracts toads.

How can I catch them?

You might want to know right away that, contrary to what many people believe, toads can't give you warts! Still, it's good to be cautious when handling these critters. The swelling behind each eye is a gland that secretes a bad-tasting substance. This is a great defense mechanism! When a predator picks a toad up in its mouth, it spits the critter out quickly because of the awful taste. This substance is not poisonous or harmful to humans in any way, but if you handle a toad and then rub your eyes, you'll feel a stinging sensation. You might also forget and put your fingers in your mouth . . . YUCK! It's important to wash your hands after handling any animal to avoid the germs that they may carry.

For catching and transporting your toad visitor, any small container will do. Fill it with a handful of grass and leaves and add a cover with holes so that the toad can't jump out. Try to get the toad to hop into the container, then quickly close the lid.

How can I keep them?

Toads generally do well in captivity if properly cared for. However, to be fair to your wild critter, don't keep it longer than a few weeks. You can keep your toad in a cardboard box or a small plastic or glass aquarium. Make sure it's large enough for the toad to hop around. If you have more than one toad, be sure their home is large enough. To make your container into a woodland terrarium, sprinkle about one inch (2.5 cm) of gravel on the bottom of the tank. The small rocks will hold excess water so that the soil won't get too soggy. Put at least two inches (5.08 cm) of soil on top of the gravel. Add a small piece of wood, a log, or some bark and a few dried leaves for the toad to burrow under. Unless you have a very tall box or aquarium, more than two feet (61 cm), for instance,

Woodland terrarium

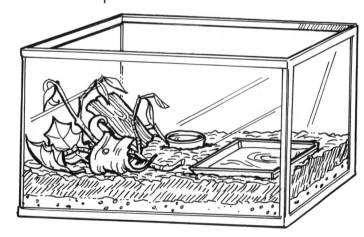

use a lid, such as a small screen or heavy wire mesh. Provide a water dish; a small aluminum baking pan works well. Bury the pan or dish in the soil so that your toad won't turn it over, and change the water daily. Toads don't drink water, but they will soak in the pan now and then to keep moist. Sprinkle or spray the soil daily with enough water to keep it damp but not wet. Include a small feeding dish for the toad's food. If you place the live prey directly on the soil, it may burrow under!

What should I feed them?

Your toad may not eat for a day or two as it gets used to its new home. If your toad goes more than three days without eating, however, set it free so it won't starve. Each toad is an individual, and another toad may adapt more successfully to captivity. Toads usually eat any small, moving creature—remember, it will be interested only in live prey. Food for your toad could include earthworms, crickets, caterpillars, ants, moths, flies, or beetles. Earthworms are the easiest to find, especially if you have access to a garden or a compost heap. Dig for them after a rainfall, when they come closer to the earth's surface.

Finding food for your toad can be pretty time-consuming. You might find it much easier to buy mealworms and crickets from a pet store. You also might be able to trick your toad into eating hamburger. Attach a tiny piece of raw hamburger to a toothpick. Dangle it in front of the toad. You may have to try this several times, but with luck, the toad's super-fast tongue will grab it faster than you can see it happening! *Be sure to wash your hands immediately after handling raw meat.* Feed your toad at least three times a week—or every day if it's got a hearty appetite.

Toad Observations

As you observe your toad, watch how it hunts. How does its tongue move when it nabs its prey? What happens when your toad swallows? How does your toad use its front feet to help it to eat prey such as worms?

You will find answers to these questions in the rest of the chapter, but be a nature detective and try to discover some of the answers through your own investigations.

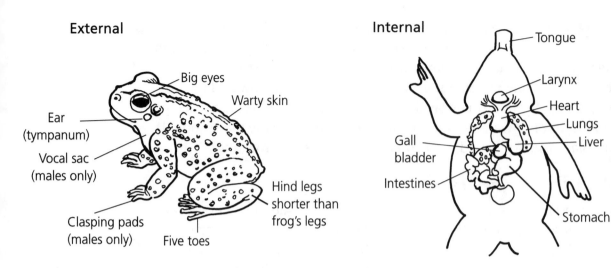

External

Big eyes

Warty skin

Ear
(tympanum)

Vocal sac
(males only)

Clasping pads
(males only)

Five toes

Hind legs
shorter than
frog's legs

Internal

Tongue

Larynx

Heart

Lungs

Liver

Gall
bladder

Intestines

Stomach

The anatomy of the toad. Look for these body parts:

Tympanum: The external eardrum. It leads to the middle ear, where sound vibrations are transferred to the inner ear.

Vocal sac: The sac in which sound is produced in male toads and frogs. It swells enormously when these animals call to attract a mate.

Hind legs: These back legs enable the toad to hop forward, but not as far as frogs.

Clasping pads: These horned pads on the thumb and index finger help the male to clasp the female during breeding.

Find out More about Toads

What's the difference between a frog and a toad?

Toads and frogs have many things in common, but let's compare their differences:

	Toad	Frog
Skin	Dry, warty, usually brown	Smooth and slimy, often green
Body	Fat with short legs	Skinny with long legs
Habitat	Usually on land	In water and land
Reproduction	Lays eggs in strings	Lays eggs in stacks
Transportation	Hopping or walking	Jumping and leaping
Hunting	Usually at night	Usually in the daytime

How are frogs and toads the same?

Most frogs and toads prefer moist habitats, although frogs must have water to live in. Both breathe air through lungs. Like all amphibians, they are both **cold-blooded** creatures. That means their body temperature depends on their surroundings. Most frogs and toads lay their eggs in water, where they hatch into tadpoles in early spring or summer. Both of these amphibians are **carnivorous** (meat-eating), feeding mainly on worms, insects, and spiders. They are both very important in controlling insect pests in gardens and near human habitats.

How long toads live?

Depending on the species, from four to fifteen years. The common European toad may live up to forty years!

Where do toads go in winter?

In colder climates, toads hibernate in winter and find cozy burrows under rocks, dead leaves, or rotten logs. A toad in hibernation does not eat or move. Even its heart beats more slowly, and its body becomes as cold as its surroundings. However, if it's protected, it will survive to greet the warmth of spring.

How does a toad eat?

Toads eat several thousand insects a month, and they will never eat anything that doesn't move. Since a toad's eyesight is not good, it won't start to stalk prey until it is almost within tongue-snapping range. Then, with amazing speed, the toad whips out its sticky tongue, and the prey is flicked into its mouth. The tongue is fastened to the front of the lower jaw.

Why does my toad close its eyes when it swallows?

When a toad swallows, its eyes press down into the upper part of its mouth. This helps in pushing the food down its throat.

How does a toad eat larger prey?

When a toad eats larger prey such as an earthworm, it stuffs the worm into its mouth using its front feet (like hands) to get a better grip. It continues stuffing until the worm disappears with one final gulp!

Why does a toad have so many warts?

A toad's warts contain glands that secrete an oily substance to keep its skin moist. This keeps it from losing moisture in dry conditions. Remember, you can't get warts from a toad!

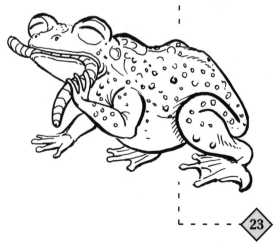

How do toads protect themselves?

Since toads are mostly dull brown, they blend in with their surroundings of dirt and leaves easily. This **camouflage** is a good defense. A toad sometimes plays dead when it's attacked. Some toads inflate their bodies with air to look bigger than a predator.

What are the predators of toads?

The hognose snake eats many toads because it's not affected by the toad's poison. Skunks and many birds, such as crows and some kinds of hawks, prey on toads and don't seem to be bothered by the poison, either!

Do toads communicate with each other?

Yes. Many species of toads have their own calls. Male toads have louder voices than females, but some have no voices at all. Toads' sounds include croaking, whistling, chirping, trilling, and other noisy carrying-ons! Males sing to females to attract them to the ponds to breed.

How do toads reproduce?

After breeding in the spring and summer, the female toad lays her eggs in a pond in one or two gel-like strings. The eggs look like strings of beads. They hatch into free-swimming tadpoles in 3 to 12 days, depending on the species and the water temperature.

How do the tadpoles become toads?

The little tadpoles eat constantly for forty to seventy days. At this time, they look like fish, and many of them are eaten by other pond creatures. The tadpole then goes through a life cycle called **metamorphosis.** It grows legs, absorbs its tail, and eventually leaves its watery home. On land, its diet changes from algae and other pond plants to insects and other small creatures.

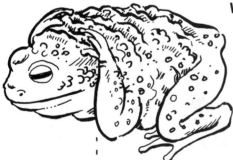

Why is my toad shedding its skin?

The dry skin of a toad doesn't stretch, so the toad must shed it now and then in order to grow. This is called **molting.** If you are lucky enough to observe this, you will notice that the skin splits down its back. The toad twists its body and wriggles to get loose. Then it tugs and sucks the old skin into its mouth and swallows it! It hops away in a brand-new suit! Young toadlets shed many times.

Do toads have ears?

Just behind the eye is a large, noticeable eardrum (tympanum). From the eardrum, the middle ear cavity transfers sound vibrations to the inner ear.

Toad Investigations

Alone or Together?

Ask:

Do toads like one another's company, or do they prefer to be alone?

Hypothesize:

From what you have observed and learned about your toads, make a prediction about their sociability.

Procedure:

1. Make a chart like this one:

Interval	Together	Apart
After 15 mins.		
After 30 mins.		
After 45 mins.		
After 60 mins.		
After 75 mins.		
After 90 mins.		
After 105 mins.		
After 120 mins.		

> **You will need:**
>
> a large box or plastic storage container (with high sides, so the toads can't escape)
>
> at least 2 toads
>
> paper and pencil

2. Place your toads in the empty container.
3. Observe their behavior for an extended period (at least 2 hours). You don't have to watch constantly, but check the toads at 15-minute intervals.
4. At each 15-minute interval, note whether the toads are together or apart. If you are experimenting with more than two toads, note this on your chart.
5. You might want to try this for several days to see whether your results change.

Results:

What did you observe? Were the toads together or apart more frequently?

Conclusions:

Can you draw any conclusions about whether toads do or do not prefer the company of other toads? Scientific studies indicate that toads generally avoid one another. Did your investigation support this?

Think about it:

Would the results be different if the toads were attracted to one another (male and female)? Why? How do the toads behave with one another in your woodland terrarium?

Food on the Move

Ask:

Will a toad eat both live and dead prey? What kind of prey movement attracts its attention first?

Hypothesize:

From what you have learned about toads' feeding habits, make a prediction.

Procedure:

1. Place a toad in a small container with both live and dead prey. Put in at least three live prey items.
2. Observe the toad to see whether:
   - the toad first eats the prey that is moving most
   - the toad first eats the prey that moves only slightly
   - the toad eats dead prey

Results:

What did you observe? How many times did you observe the toad catching its prey?

Conclusions:

Can you arrive at any conclusions based on your observations? Do you need additional trials to learn more? You have learned that

---

You will need:

a toad

both live and dead prey items (such as live and dead worms or live and dead beetles)

a small container

toads will not eat prey that is not moving. Did your investigation support this fact?

Think about it:

Do you think it benefits toads to eat only moving prey? Why or why not? What other creatures require their prey to be alive? Consider other amphibians, mammals, reptiles, birds, fish, and insects. Do you know which creatures will eat both live and dead prey?

INVESTIGATION 3

Favorite Foods

Ask:

Do toads prefer certain foods?

Hypothesize:

Based on your previous observations of your toad and what you've learned about toads' eating habits, make a prediction.

You will need:

a toad

several live prey items, such as a worm, cricket, grasshopper, mealworm, fly, beetle, caterpillar, or ant

a flat container

paper and pencil

Procedure:

1. Place the toad in the flat container with several of the prey items.
2. As you observe the toad, note the following:
   ◆ Which prey does the toad eat first?
   ◆ Which prey does it eat next? (if it has a big appetite!)
   ◆ Which prey was moving most when the toad ate it?
3. Write down the information you gather.
4. Try this investigation on at least two different days to compare results.

Results:

What did you observe about your toad's food preferences?

Conclusions:

What conclusions can you make from your observations? Did your toad seem to be affected more by prey movement than by food choice? Do you need to observe more before you can make conclusions?

Think about it:

Scientific studies indicate that toads will eat just about anything that's moving! Describe an experiment that might produce more insight about toad food preferences. It might be difficult, even for scientists, to make conclusions about this question. Why?

Toad Activities

ACTIVITY 1

Toad Taming

While toads may not be soft and cuddly like some small mammals, they can become surprisingly tame. Try this activity to see whether your toad can learn to recognize you (or at least your hand)!

You will need:

a toad visitor and its woodland habitat

prey items (whatever live critters you can find)

Procedure:

1. To tame your toad, you must be both patient and gentle. For several days, pick up your toad frequently (but gently) so that it will get used to being handled. In the woodland terrarium, place the prey item right in front of the toad each time you feed it. Move your hand away (but still in the terrarium). Do this for several days.

2. Begin moving your hand closer each time you feed the toad. Don't rush this. Your toad needs time to learn that your hand is not a predator!

3. Once your toad will eat when your hand is nearby, place a prey item (non-hopping) on the palm of your hand or hold it with your fingers so that it can show movement. Try this several times until the toad either hops onto your palm to eat or takes the prey from your fingers. The taming process may take two or more weeks. Some toads (like people) are shy and may not like human contact. It's great fun if your toad gets to know and trust you!

Toad Training

Now that your toad knows you a little better, you might want to see just how smart it is!

Procedure:

1. In full view of your toad, bury some worms in the soil of the terrarium. Then loosen the soil to reveal the worms to the toad. Remove your hand. If it's hungry, your toad will probably eat the worms quickly, before they burrow into the soil.
2. Repeat this several times in the same spot. Your toad should come to expect that when your hand appears, food will follow, and it will quickly move to the soil area when your hand appears in the terrarium. Of course, this may have more to do with trained learning behavior than IQ, but it does demonstrate that this little critter can learn.

You will need:

a toad and its
   woodland habitat

worms

Toad Abode

Procedure:

1. Choose a spot in your backyard where you might expect to find toads.
2. Put the pot upside down with an edge resting on a rock (so that the toad can go into the pot to hide).
3. Fill the saucer with water and place it next to the pot.
4. Check for visitors, especially at night.
5. If no toads visit the "abode" on their own, look for a toad who might welcome such a cozy home! If you find one, introduce it to your abode. This one might decide it's quite a comfy place to live. Did you get any visitors other than toads? If so, make observations.

You will need:

a medium-size clay
   pot

a clay saucer or
   any other large
   saucer

your backyard

3 Wriggling Worms

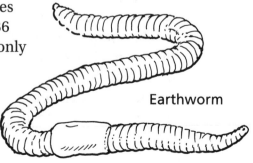

Earthworm Basics

If you are thinking of skipping this chapter (*eeewww*, worms are gross!), please don't. I promise that once you begin to learn about these interesting creatures, you'll be hooked (sorry!) on keeping some of your own. You may even want to start a worm farm!

There are lots of reasons to be amazed by worms. Did you ever wonder how a creature with no arms or legs can tunnel so deeply into the ground, as far down as 8 feet (2.4 m)? You may have heard that worms benefit the soil in many ways, but do you know how or why? If you read on, you may even begin to like picking up worms!

There are many kinds of worms . . . about 40,000 species in the world. We will be learning about the common earthworm, one of the 8,500 kinds of **segmented** worms. These worms have a body made up of many small segments, or rings. The segmented worms are called **annelids.** There are more than 3,000 species of earthworms in the world, and these range from tiny, inch-long worms to a species in Australia that can grow to 12 feet (36 cm)! Most earthworms, however, are only a few inches long.

Earthworm

Where can I find them?

You can find earthworms fairly easily wherever you live: in hot, cold, wet, or dry climates. The very best places to look are where the soil is loose, damp, and "airy," such as in a garden, under leaf litter (old leaves), or in compost heaps. It's harder to find them in sandy or very dry, packed soil. After a rainfall, or when the earth is moist, worms often come to the top of the soil, so try to search then. If you can't find the worms, look for their holes and the small bits of soil they leave after burrowing. Don't stomp your feet where you're searching. Worms can sense vibrations and will burrow deeper into the soil.

How can I catch them?

The only equipment you'll need to get worms is a shovel, trowel, or hand garden fork for digging and a container to hold the worms. If you are keeping the worms for observation, it's best if you set up your worm habitat before you bring your worms home. A garden fork works best to loosen the soil. If you're not careful with a shovel, you may chop some worms! It's best to dig up a big chunk of soil and break it apart with your hands. If you still think worms are icky to handle, you can pick them up with a plastic spoon. Collect up to 10 worms for a one-gallon (3.8-liter) container. Larger containers (such as an aquarium tank) can hold more.

How can I keep them?

You will need a clear glass or plastic container so that you can observe your worms. The larger the container the better, but even a two-quart size will do. It's best if the worms can burrow down at least 10 inches (25 cm). You might use a fish tank, a gallon pickle jar, or a plastic terrarium.

In a separate container, make a mixture of light soil. The best is dark brown or black, such as garden or potting soil. Add pieces of dead and decaying leaves. Maple is best, and avoid oak, since worms dislike oak. Dampen the soil mixture. Since worms love coffee grounds, you can add one to two tablespoons now and again every few days. Put a layer of stones or gravel on the bottom of the container for drainage, then pack the soil firmly into the container with about a 2-inch (5-cm) space on top.

Now place your worms on top and cover the container with nylon, mesh, or screening so they won't climb out. Earthworms don't like

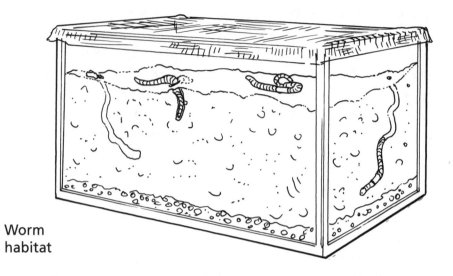

Worm
habitat

light, so cover the container with tin foil or black paper. Place them in a cool dark place, away from radiators and windows. Be sure to keep the soil moist but not so wet that it becomes muddy. (A spray bottle works well.) It may take a few days before the worms start burrowing.

What should I feed them?

Worms eat rotted leaves and plant material, so be sure to add some a couple of times each week. You can also try grass, green leafy vegetables, and potato peels. Your observations will tell you which foods your earthworms prefer. You can tempt their tastebuds with a variety of other foods such as orange rinds, cucumbers, oatmeal, apples, and celery, to name just a few. Be sure to remove uneaten foods before they rot. Earthworms also like coffee grounds and cornmeal, but mix these in the top soil so that you won't disturb their burrows.

Earthworm Observations

There are so many observations you can make about earthworms! How do they move? When are they stretched out and when do they curl up? What do they do when they meet each other? What are their favorite foods? If you don't want to keep them in a worm habitat, you can simply observe them where they live outside. Use a magnifying glass for closer investigations, and try observing them at night with a flashlight.

The anatomy of the earthworm. Look for these body parts:

Clitellum: the swollen band or ring around the earthworm's body that produces the mucus needed for fertilization.

Setae: four pairs of short, bristly hairs on each segment of the worm that help it to move through the soil.

Body segments: the space between two rings.

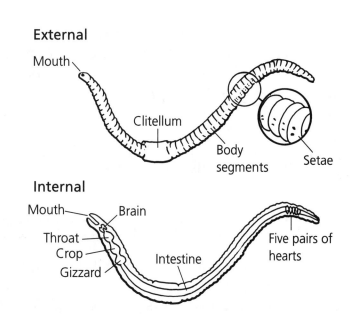

External

Mouth
Clitellum
Body segments
Setae

Internal

Mouth
Brain
Throat
Crop
Gizzard
Intestine
Five pairs of hearts

Find out More about Earthworms

Why does a worm have stripes around its body?

These stripes are really rings that divide the worm's body into segments. A segment is a space between two rings. Most earthworms have 100 to 200 segments.

Which end is a worm's head?

Find the **clitellum** (the light-colored band around an adult worm's body). This band is closer to the worm's head. Watch the worm move. The front end (head) moves first . . . unless it's crawling backward!

What and how does a worm eat?

You've learned that worms eat decayed leaves and other plant matter. However, when there's not enough plant material around, worms actually swallow the soil. The soil has bits of animal and plant material mixed in with little stones. This passes through their bodies into the **gizzard,** where it is ground up. This fine pulp is then changed into tiny pellets called **castings,** which are eliminated from the **anus.** Look for these castings to locate worms. Earthworms can also pull leaves right into their burrows!

How does a worm move without legs?

Watch the worm move. Notice how it stretches and then pulls its body up. The worm is so flexible because it has no backbone. Its movements are made possible by two sets of

muscles. One set (the **longitudinal muscles**) runs lengthwise along the body. These draw the body up by **contracting,** or squeezing together. The worm's body now looks short and plump. The other set (the **circular muscles**) circles the body. When they contract, the body becomes long and thin. The worm moves along the soil by alternating these two sets of muscles—using first one set and then the other.

How an earthworm moves

Why does my worm's body feel bristly?

Earthworms have bristles, or tiny spines, called **setae** on each segment, two pair on the bottom and one on each side. Moving these bristles forward and backward helps the worm to crawl and to hold onto surfaces.

Can a worm protect itself?

Worms protect themselves in several ways. Their color helps them to blend into their surroundings (camouflage), and they can burrow and hide from aboveground predators. However, they don't have much protection against moles and other underground hunters.

What are other worm predators?

Birds, such as robins, love to eat earthworms. Toads, salamanders, shrews, and even skunks like to eat them, too. Fishermen are hunters of worms, also! In spite of their many enemies, there are still enough earthworms to populate the soil of the world!

If a worm is cut in half, will it grow a new half?

Well, not if it's cut exactly in half. If the worm is cut before the first 12 segments or after the last 4 or 5, it will be able to grow new parts, or **regenerate.** If it's split right down the center, it won't live.

Why is a worm slimy?

Mucus glands in a worm's skin produce slime, which helps the worm to wriggle easily through the soil. More important, the slime keeps the worm moist so that it can breathe through its skin.

Can a worm see, hear, or smell?

An earthworm doesn't have senses as we do, but it has nerve cells that provide sensation. It reacts to light using the light-sensitive cells in its front end. Though the worm can't hear, it can sense vibrations that come through the earth. It doesn't have a nose or lungs but instead takes in air through its skin. Try some of the investigations in this chapter to learn some of an earthworm's special talents!

Does a worm have a brain and a heart?

Yes. The tiny brain is in the front of its body. Though it can't think as we do, the brain collects messages from nerve cells all over the worm's body and allows it to react to its surroundings. The earthworm has five pairs of hearts, which are actually enlarged blood vessels located in its last few segments. These "hearts" pump blood throughout its body.

How can you tell a male from a female worm?

You can't! Earthworms, like snails, are hermaphrodites. This means that each earthworm is both a male and a female! Each worm can produce both eggs and sperm to fertilize the eggs. This helps worms considerably, since their burrowing prevents them from meeting often.

Then how do worms reproduce?

Two worms will lie head to tail to fertilize each other's eggs. The eggs are laid in the soil in sacs, each of which holds four developing worms. The tiny eggs hatch in about a month, and the baby worms come out looking like rice grains that are usually purple or red. Look for them in the leaf litter where you find worms.

How long do earthworms live?

They may live for several years when raised by people, but in their natural habitats they probably only live for a year or so.

Why do earthworms come out after it rains?

No one is sure why. The rain may flood their burrows, or the water may keep air out of the soil, forcing the worm to come up for air.

What are night crawlers?

The night crawler is a common garden earthworm that comes up for food at dusk or at night. To get food, it keeps its hind end in the burrow and stretches out to find leaves or other food. Then it pulls the food down with it. Fishermen hunt for night crawlers because they are often very large and make good bait.

How do earthworms help the soil?

Earthworms **aerate** or let air into the soil with their burrowing action. This lets water seep deeper into the ground. Their castings (waste products) enrich the soil, and good soil may have as many as one million worms per acre!

Earthworm Investigations

Wet or Dry?

You will need:

a cookie sheet or other waterproof surface

paper towels

one or more earthworms

Ask:

Do worms prefer damp or dry places?

Hypothesize:

From what you know about worms, make a prediction about this.

Procedure:

1. Wet a paper towel and wring it out so it's not sopping wet. Place it on one side of the cookie sheet.
2. Place a dry paper towel on the other half of the surface so that the sides of the towels are overlapping.
3. Place a worm on either the damp towel or the dry towel. If you have several worms, place an equal number on each towel.
4. Observe whether the worms stay on the towel they started on or move to the other one.
5. Try this experiment several times and record your results. You can devise your own chart or use one like this:

Trials	1	2	3	4	5	6
Worms on wet towel						
Worms on dry towel						

Results:

Where did the majority of the worms go or stay?

Conclusions:

In the wild, worms prefer moist habitats. Did your investigation confirm this preference? If not, what do you think happened? Could you draw any conclusions about the question asked?

Think about it:

Would you obtain similar results if you used soil (wet and dry) in your experiment? Try it and see. Why is moisture necessary to a worm's survival?

Light or Dark?

Ask:

How do different parts of an earthworm's body react to light?

Hypothesize:

From what you know about the worm's behavior and its light-sensitive cells, make a prediction.

Procedure:

1. Tape a piece of dark paper firmly over the lens of the flashlight. You can also cut a circular piece of cardboard to fit snugly into the head of the flashlight.
2. Make a pin-size hole in the paper or cardboard.
3. Place the worm on the damp towel.
4. Darken the room (or do this outside at night).
5. Focus the beam of light from the flashlight along the sides of the worm. Move the light toward the back end and then the front.
6. Repeat this procedure with at least 4 more worms.
7. Record your observations on a chart like this one. Describe how each worm reacted when you shined the light on both its head and tail. For instance, did it wriggle, crawl away, or stay still?

Worm	Reaction: Head	Reaction: Tail
1		
2		
3		
4		
5		

Results:

Did each worm react to light on its back end? Its front end? Neither end?

You will need:

a flashlight

dark paper or cardboard

a damp paper towel

5 or more earthworms

tape

a large safety pin

Conclusions:

Were the reactions the same in each worm? If they differed, describe how. Most worms react to light by wriggling when the light is focused on their front end. Did your investigation support this?

Think about it:

You learned that the worm's sensory organs are located in its head. How do the light-sensitive cells help it to find and come to the surface of the ground from its burrow?

Touch Test

You will need:

a worm

a damp paper towel

a blade of grass, pencil, or other light object

Ask:

How does an earthworm react to touch?

Hypothesize:

Make a prediction about an earthworm's touch sensitivity.

Procedure:

1. Place the worm on the paper towel.
2. Touch it very lightly with your finger, a blade of grass, a pencil, or another light object, first on its tail, then on its middle, and finally on its head. Be gentle. More than a light touch could be painful to this tiny creature.
3. Note how the worm reacts to each touch.

Results:

Which parts of the worm were most sensitive to touch?

Conclusions:

A worm's head is extremely sensitive to touch. Did your experiment indicate this?

Think about it:

If a bird touches a worm's head, the worm will suddenly contract (squeeze up). How could this reaction help the worm to survive? Human bodies also differ in their sensitivity to touch. Pinch the skin on your elbow very hard. Now pinch the top of your thigh just as hard. Which area is more sensitive? Your thigh has many nerve endings and is probably much more sensitive. Why do our elbows benefit from being less sensitive than fattier body parts? (That is, unless you whack your "funny bone"!)

Earthworm Activities

ACTIVITY
1

Earthworm Diorama

Design and make a realistic model of an earthworm and provide it with a shoebox habitat (diorama). This is a great activity to do if you can't make a live worm habitat or if it's too cold outside and worms are not available.

Procedure:

1. Design your worm out of modeling clay using the worm-body-parts diagram. Do you remember what color the clitellum is?

2. Using a clay modeling or butter knife, carve as many segments as possible on your worm. Why can't you make all of them? About how many segments does an earthworm have?

3. Cut the broom bristles into tiny pieces for the setae. Again, you won't be able to provide all of them. How many setae are on each segment? Where are they?

4. If using self-drying clay, paint your worm when the clay is dry.

5. Stand the shoebox on its side and add the natural materials. Make your worm's surroundings as scenic as you like.

You will need:

modeling or self-drying clay

a diagram of worm body parts

clay modeling tools or a butter knife.

1 or 2 broom bristles

scissors

poster or other paints (for clay if using self-drying)

habitat materials such as soil, dead leaves, moss, twigs, and stones

6. Add your worm and display. This is one worm that isn't slimy!

They All Add Up

The population growth rate of earthworms is amazing!
Each worm can lay two to three cocoons per week, and each cocoon can have up to four worms. Try these math problems to see how many worms can multiply from just one little worm! The answers are on the bottom of the page, but don't peek until you've done the math!

1. If a worm lays 3 cocoons a week, and 4 babies emerge from each cocoon, how many worms will there be in 3 weeks?
2. If 2 worms lay 2 cocoons in one week, and 2 babies emerge from each cocoon, how many worms will there be in 5 weeks?
3. If 20 worms each produce 30 babies, how many worms are there all together?
4. If one worm makes 468 babies a year, how many babies will 50 worms make in a year?

Answers:

1. $3 \times 4 \times 3 = 36$ worms
2. $2 \times 2 \times 5 = 20$ worms
3. $20 \times 30 = 600$ worms
4. $468 \times 50 = 23,400$ worms!

Worm Fiddling

Try this amazing way to get worms out of their
burrows, even in the daytime!

Procedure:

1. On the unpointed stake, have an adult make deep notches
   about 5 inches (12 cm) apart.
2. Bring your stakes to an area of damp soil (or wet the soil the
   day before). Look especially in places where you see worm
   holes.
3. Use a hammer or rock to pound the pointed stake into the
   ground.
4. Pull the notched edge of the other stake back and forth across
   the side of the one in the ground in a sawing motion. It may
   take a while to get the knack of this, but keep trying. Can you feel
   the vibrations? So can the worms!
5. If there are worms in the ground in that area, they will come
   right out of their burrows!

You will need:

help from an adult

two 18-inch
   (46-cm) stakes
   about 2 inches
   (5 cm) wide (one
   stake must be
   pointed at the
   end)

a hammer or a rock

4 Chirping Crickets

Cricket Basics

You are probably already familiar with the chirping sound of the cricket. Have you heard a cricket's call outdoors . . . in the woods or fields, on a city sidewalk, or in your backyard? Has a cricket visited your home in the fall, when it seeks refuge from cooler weather? Many people have heard crickets, but not as many have seen them, since they are shy and sensitive insects. In this chapter, we will get up close and personal with this charming bug. We won't be among the first to admire them. Over a thousand years ago, Chinese royalty kept crickets in fancy golden cages. Poor people kept them, too, but in simple clay cages. Crickets are still kept in China and Japan, where they are greatly admired for their songs and as symbols of good luck.

Like other insects, crickets are **arthropods.** Arthropods have joined legs and no backbones. Their bodies are segmented into parts: the head, the **thorax** (where the legs and wings are attached), and the **abdomen** (the rear section).

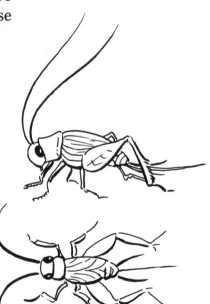

Field cricket

Crickets belong to the insect family **Gryllidae.** They can be found all over the world, in many different kinds of habitats. There are many species or kinds, but we will focus on the field cricket, which is easy to find and catch.

I'm sure you'll be fascinated by them. Happy cricketeering!

Where can I find them?

The best times to look for field crickets are the late summer and fall. The field cricket is black or brown and about one inch (2.5 cm) long. Look for crickets under rocks, boards, leafy plants, or in decaying logs, or in other hiding places. You can also find a cricket by trying to follow its song, but this method often proves to be frustrating. As soon as you seem to be getting close, the cricket wisely stops chirping! If you have a backyard, another method is to gather a pile of grass clippings. If you keep the pile damp, crickets may gather there. If you have no luck finding them, you can buy them in bait stores and pet shops. They're very inexpensive. When you have finished observing them, be sure to release them in a grassy habitat so they can find a new home.

How can I catch them?

On your cricket hunt, bring a plastic catching container (about the size of a peanut butter jar) and another jar for holding the insect. When you find a cricket, pop the catching jar on top of the cricket. Be careful not to injure its legs. Keep your hand on top of the jar and slide it away as you carefully transfer it into the holding jar. You can also slide a piece of cardboard under the catching jar and then transfer the cricket directly into a jar or terrarium. You can catch crickets with your hands, but these other methods are usually safer for these fragile creatures.

How can I keep them?

You can keep your crickets in a large plastic jar (glass is okay but may break if you're not careful) or a small glass or plastic terrarium. Cover the bottom of the container with about two inches (5 cm) of damp soil. Add a piece of bark or wood and a rock or leaf for the cricket to burrow under. Include a toilet paper roll for it to hide in. For deluxe accommodations in a terrarium, include four attached sections of an egg carton (with openings cut out). If you're using a jar, cover the top with mesh or nylon fastened with a rubber band; for a terrarium, use the lid if it's equipped with one or a piece of cheesecloth so that the cricket can't jump out. Clean the habitat often if you keep the cricket for more than a few days so that uneaten food and droppings will not accumulate. The more the merrier when it comes to cricket watching, but if you have just one, you're still lucky.

Deluxe cricket habitat

What should I feed them?

Feed your crickets grass, green leaves, lettuce, carrots, moistened bread and cereal, and cut-up pieces of fruit. You can even experiment with tiny pieces of meat or dry dog food. If you have more than one cricket, they are less likely to fight if they have protein. Keep the food in a small container and remove old food, being sure to add fresh items daily. Spray the container with water every day or put water in a bottle cap. (Crickets may drown in a water dish.) The soil should be kept moist by spraying it every other day or so.

Cricket Observations

When you watch your cricket, try to observe the following: How does it move? Hop? Walk? What behaviors do you observe? Hiding? Eating Fighting? Chirping? What different body parts does it have, and how does it use them?

The anatomy of the cricket. Look for these body parts:

Cerci: A pair of feelers at the rear of the insect's abdomen. There are about 750 hairs on each cercus.

Compound eyes: Tiny lenses in the eyes of some insects and animals that have many different sides and surfaces.

Ovipositor: A stalk-like tube at the end of a female's abdomen used to lay eggs in the soil.

Palpi: Feelers on the mouth parts used to feel for food.

Two pairs of wings: The cricket's top set of wings overlaps the other when closed.

Jumping legs: These strong, muscular legs help the cricket to jump a long way.

External

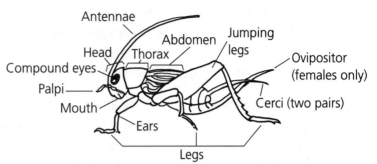

Internal

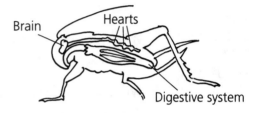

Find out More about Crickets

Do crickets have ears?

Yes, but they are in a strange place, at least to us! The ears are under the knees of the cricket's front legs! Each ear is a tiny hole with a tight membrane or cover called the **tympanal organs.**

Where do field crickets live in the wild?

Field crickets are common in meadows, woods, and backyards. They live anywhere they can find food, including busy towns and cities. They even invite themselves into our homes when the weather turns cool. Field crickets are also known to live in tiny tunnels in the ground.

What do field crickets eat in the wild?

Field crickets feed on plants and plant material, such as fruits or seeds, and sometimes small insects.

Do crickets have teeth?

No, but they have strong jaws to cut up the small insects and leaves they eat.

Do crickets sing because they're happy?

No, at least not happy as we know it! Only the male cricket sings, and the main reason is **courtship:** He wants to attract a female mate. The cricket also sings to let other crickets know where he is and to warn other males to stay out of his territory. They will fight any who trespass! Scientists record cricket songs to try to tell one kind of song from another.

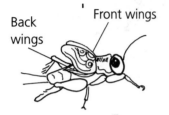

Back wings

Front wings

A male cricket uses his front wings to "sing."

How does a male cricket sing?

When a male cricket begins to sing, he lifts his top wings and holds them over his back. He draws the rough edge of the front wing, called the **file,** across a ridge, or **scraper,** on the other front wing. This produces the buzzing sound that is cricket song.

When do crickets sing most often?

Most crickets sing at night, but the field cricket also sings in the daytime.

Will my female crickets lay eggs?

If you have males, they may! Be sure to provide one inch (25 mm) of sand for egg laying.

What do baby crickets look like?

Newly hatched crickets, or **nymphs,** look like tiny adults without wings.

How does a nymph grow?

Like other insects, the cricket has an outer shell called an **exoskeleton.** It sheds this exoskeleton so that its body can grow. This shedding is called molting. A cricket molts several times before it becomes an adult.

Can crickets fly?

Most species can't. A few can become slightly airborne.

What are the predators of crickets?

Many critters like to eat crickets, including snakes, birds, lizards, mantises, and toads.

How does a cricket protect itself?

A cricket's best defense against predators is to hide. Once it's found, it can only try to hop away. Even those species that fly can't lift off into the air high enough to escape a predator.

How do male crickets fight?

Male crickets may kick, butt heads, and wrestle with their opponents. The fight is over when the loser retreats! If your male crickets fight, keep the one that seems to start most of the fights in a separate container.

Cricket Investigations

Cricket Sociability

Ask:

Do crickets prefer to live alone or together?

Hypothesize:

From what you have observed and learned about your crickets so far, make a prediction about their sociability.

Procedure:

1. Choose the type of cricket house you want to make. If you are using baking cups, cut a small opening in one side large enough so that the cricket can enter. If you are using milk cartons, cut off the top pouring section and make a doorway on one of the sides. If you are using toilet paper rolls, cut them in half.

> **You will need:**
>
> 2 or more crickets
>
> cricket houses: paper cupcake baking cups *or* small milk cartons *or* toilet paper rolls cut in half (one for each cricket)
>
> a box big enough to fit all the cricket houses inside
>
> sand
>
> scissors
>
> paper and pencil
>
> permanent marker (optional)
>
> trial chart

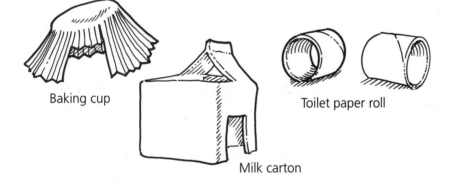

Baking cup

Milk carton

Toilet paper roll

2. Number each cricket house. (You may have to use permanent marker on the milk carton.)
3. Put a layer of sand on the bottom of the box and put your crickets in the box.
4. Observe the behavior of the crickets and check the houses at 5 minute intervals.

5. Record how many crickets are in each house on a chart like this:

Interval	Number of Crickets in:				
	House 1	House 2	House 3	House 4	House 5
After 5 mins.					
After 10 mins.					
After 15 mins.					
After 20 mins.					
After 25 mins.					
After 30 mins.					
After 35 mins.					
After 40 mins.					
After 45 mins.					
After 50 mins.					
After 55 mins.					
After 60 mins.					

Results:

How many crickets were in each house during each 5-minute interval?

Conclusions:

Can you make any conclusions based on the crickets' behavior with one another? Did your experiment support the theory that crickets usually prefer to live alone?

Think about it:

Did any of the crickets chirp? If so, did you find the chirping cricket in the company of another? What do you think was happening? (Or about to happen!)

Cricket Song

Ask:

Who's singing that song?

Hypothesize:

Predict which of your crickets will chirp or sing.

Procedure:

1. Study these illustrations so that you can identify and select the crickets for this experiment.

You will need:

several crickets of different sizes and both sexes

4 or more small food jars, all the same size

sand

a damp cotton ball or a damp wadded-up paper towel

cricket food

pieces of nylon or mesh and elastic bands to cover jars

masking tape

marker

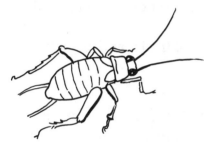

Immature male (small wings)

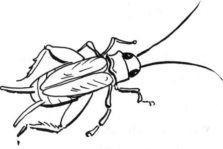

Mature male (large wings)

Immature female (ovipositor and small wings)

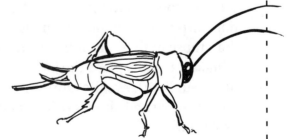

Mature female (ovipositor and large wings)

2. Tape a small piece of masking tape on each jar and number them.
3. Add sand, the damp cotton ball or paper towel, and fill the jars with food.
4. After choosing crickets, pair them in a variety of ways and place them in the jars. For example, you could put two adult males together, or one adult male and one adult female. Maybe you'd like to try putting one immature female and one adult male in the same jar, or two adult females. You can also put one male in a jar by himself.
5. Arrange the jars one foot (30 cm) apart, but make sure they receive the same amount of light.
6. Walk away from the jars, but remain close enough to hear and observe.
7. If you hear a chirp, record the number of the jar and any other cricket behavior.

Results:

Which cricket or pair combinations of crickets chirped the most? Which cricket or pair combinations didn't chirp at all?

Conclusions:

Can you draw any conclusions about cricket song from this investigation? Would you get different results if you experimented with different crickets but in the same male-female representations? Do you think mating or aggression has something to do with which crickets chirp or which don't?

Think about it:

What factors in your experiment might have caused the crickets to not chirp at all? Do most animals in captivity behave differently than those in their natural surroundings? Why? If you did not get "singing" results, place the jars in a warmer area (but never in direct sunlight). Are the chirping results different? From what you have learned about crickets and warmer temperatures, explain why.

Boys Will Be Boys

Ask:

What can we observe about male crickets' reactions to each other?

Hypothesize:

From what you know about male cricket behavior, how do you think they will behave when you put them together?

Procedure:

1. Put the sand into the aquarium tank or box and place the toilet paper roll on top. (*Note:* You can reuse the habitat you've already made for your crickets, but remove all but the crickets for this investigation.)
2. Gently mark your crickets with permanent marker dots to identify them. For example, put one dot on one cricket, two dots on another.
3. Put one male cricket into the aquarium. In about 30 minutes, add the second. Observe their behavior. Describe any songs or chirping from each male.

Results:

What did you observe when you placed the two males together? Did you observe any aggressive behavior? Did they fight with one another? Was one cricket more dominant (bossier) than the other? Did either male enter the roll and then try to defend it? If both chirped, which one was the loudest? Did one of the males chirp while inside the roll? Crickets have been known to use leaves and other things in their habitats to make their chirps seem louder. Did the roll amplify the chirp (make it seem louder)?

Conclusions:

Could you draw any conclusions about cricket social behaviors from this investigation?

Think about it:

From what you have learned about cricket behavior, can you think of any of this critter's behaviors that might compare with human

> **You will need:**
>
> a 5-gallon aquarium tank or large box
>
> moist sand
>
> a toilet paper roll
>
> 2 male crickets
>
> black permanent marker

behavior? Describe both similarities and differences. Try this investigation with a variety of crickets to observe their behavior more closely.

Cricket Activities

ACTIVITY 1

Hot and Cold Crickets

Place your cricket in the refrigerator (in a jar, of course) for about 20 minutes, then take it out and observe: Is the cricket more or less active when it's cold? What does this tell you about how temperature affects cricket behavior? (*Note:* Cooling the cricket won't harm it, but make sure you remove it from the refrigerator after about 20 minutes.)

ACTIVITY 2

Jumping Jacks (and Jills)

How far can your cricket jump? Place your cricket next to a yardstick on the grass and measure the distance it jumps. Then follow the same procedure on other surfaces, such as concrete, sand, or dirt, or the floor. On which surface did it jump the farthest? Why? Most crickets can jump about 2 feet (60 cm). Did yours? If you have more than one cricket, see how far each one can jump. Do the males jump farther than the females? Do adults outjump younger crickets (immatures)? Which is your champion jumper?

ACTIVITY 3

Backyard Cricket Hunt

If you and your friends or siblings hear a cricket in your backyard, see who can find the cricket first. (You'll have an advantage since you know that the cricket will stop singing if it hears you approaching.) The first one to find the cricket's hiding place gets to catch and keep it (and show it to Auntie Sophie during lunch).

Crawly Caterpillars

5

Caterpillar Basics

There are over 200,000 species of butterflies and moths in the world. They can be found on all continents except Antarctica. These insects belong to the order **Lepidoptera.** Butterfly species include some of the largest and most beautiful insects as well as some of the smallest. An **entomologist** (a scientist who studies insects) could tell you a lot about butterflies, but you'd probably need to consult a **lepidopterist** (a scientist who studies butterflies) to find out about the rarest ones.

The caterpillar is the main feeding stage (or **larva**) in the life cycle of butterflies and moths. The adult butterfly and moth are the mating and egg-laying stage of this lovely insect. Caterpillars make one of the best "creepy-crawly" pets since they are easy to catch, feed, and keep.

Zebra caterpillar

Tent caterpillar

Elephant hawk moth caterpillar

Where can I find them?

If you live in a four-season climate, the best time to look for caterpillars is in the spring and summer. Look on leaves, branches, tree trunks, and even the ground. Find caterpillar clues such as holes in leaves and droppings (small brown bits of digested leaves called **frass**) on the leaves. Be sure to look on the undersides of leaves, too.

Most caterpillars are harmless, but don't touch the gypsy moth caterpillar. Its stinging hairs might cause a mild stinging sensation or a rash. Also, the Io moth caterpillar has spines that can give you a painful sting. It's a good idea to get a field guide to caterpillars and butterflies from the library so that you'll be able to identify what you find.

Caterpillars
to avoid

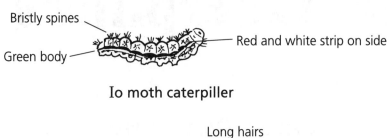

Bristly spines

Green body

Red and white strip on side

Io moth caterpiller

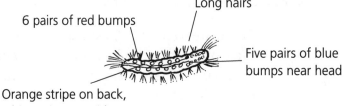

6 pairs of red bumps

Long hairs

Five pairs of blue bumps near head

Orange stripe on back, white stripes on side

Gypsy moth caterpiller

How can I catch them?

This is fairly easy! On your search, take along a small container with a lid. (A plastic one is best since it won't break.) Ask an adult to make a few holes in the lid so that the creature can breathe. This will do quite nicely until you get home and put the caterpillar into a more permanent habitat. Bring a small piece of sturdy paper (such as an index card) with you.

It's best to remove the entire leaf from the tree (or plant) where you find the caterpillar to avoid injuring it. If the caterpillar is on a branch or on the ground, remove it gently. You can also carefully try to slide the paper under the caterpillar to loosen its hold. If the creature seems steadfast, leave it be and look elsewhere!

If you found the caterpillar on a leaf or branch, take several stemmed leaves from the plant or tree home with you so that you will have a supply of what it eats. Caterpillars can be very picky eaters! If you found the caterpillar on the ground, try taking leaves from a few plants or trees nearby. Unless you know what the caterpillar eats, don't keep it for more than a day since it may starve. Experiment with a few different kinds of leaves; with a little luck, your tiny creature may choose one to eat.

How can I keep them?

If you plan to keep the caterpillar until it changes into a butterfly or moth, provide it with enough space to crawl around. A 12-by-7-inch (30-by-18-cm) terrarium with a lid is probably ample room for most species. If you will only be observing the caterpillar for a few days, a large jar will do. Place a piece of lightweight cloth or nylon stocking (not Mom's new ones!) over the top, fastened with an elastic band. Plenty of air will be able to circulate through the cloth.

Place the twig or branch with its leaves in the jar or terrarium. Put the end of the twig in a plastic pill container filled with water. If your caterpillar is small, place cotton around the top of the pill container (not touching the water) so that the caterpillar won't fall in and drown! You can also simply wrap a wet paper towel around the stem and secure it with a rubber band. Yet another method to keep the greenery fresh is to stick the twigs into a block oasis (a type of hard green sponge used for flower arranging) soaked in water.

If you have a moth caterpillar (larva), provide it with a thick layer of earth and leaves for its **cocoon** (a soft case, usually made of silk, in which moths have their **pupal stage**). A butterfly larva will need a sturdy, pencil-thick branch for its **chrysalis** (a hardened case in which butterflies have their pupal stage).

Add some small branches and rocks to provide recreation for your crawly visitor. Lightly spray water into the jar daily and replace the eaten leaves with fresh ones. Keep the container out of direct sunlight.

Caterpillar habitat

Once your caterpillar develops into a butterfly or moth, you must let it go, since they seldom survive in captivity without expert attention. Plan a farewell party: "So long . . . have a good life!"

What should I feed them?

As you have already learned, it's important to know what your caterpillar will eat. Every caterpillar species has a particular type of plant (or family of plants) with which it's associated. To keep a caterpillar for a while, you must remember the plant it was on when you collected it. As soon as most of the food plant is eaten or it starts to wilt, you must change it for fresh leaves. Are you sure you will be able to get a good supply of the food plant as your tiny pet grows? If not, let it go after one day.

Caterpillar Observations

Is your caterpillar smooth? Bumpy? Horned? Hairy? Bristly? Spiny? Notice the caterpillar's color and the type of plant it's on. Use a caterpillar guidebook to identify the species you find.

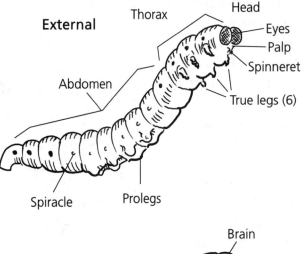

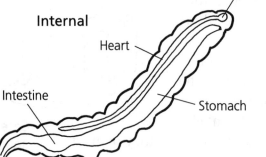

The anatomy of the caterpillar. Look for these body parts:

Mandible: Jaws used to cut off pieces of leaves or other foods.

Ocelli: Simple eyes.

Prolegs: Unjointed hind legs of a caterpillar with tiny hooks used for grasping. Also known as the clasper.

Spinneret: Produces silk to anchor caterpillar and make its cocoon.

Spiracles: Allow air in and out of the body.

True legs: Jointed legs that will also be present in the adult butterfly (or moth).

Find out More about Caterpillars

How do caterpillars grow?

Butterflies and moths lay their eggs on vegetation during the spring and summer. The tiny caterpillars that emerge eat and eat until they are ready to burst, which they nearly do! The caterpillar's skin actually splits down the back, allowing it to molt or shed its skin. After each molt, the caterpillar is bigger, and it may also change color or shape. Caterpillars make 3 to 5 molts before they are full-grown.

How does a caterpillar turn into a butterfly or moth?

This event is amazing! After its last molt, the larva or young caterpillar stops eating. A butterfly caterpillar finds a twig, branch, or other surface and weaves a silk button on the chosen spot. When it has finished weaving, it fastens itself to the button and hangs upside down from it. Then the caterpillar begins to form a chrysalis around itself. This is the pupal stage. Soon the chrysalis hardens. Instead of forming a chrysalis, moth larva spin cocoons on the ground, hidden under branches, leaves, or foliage. Now the mysterious transformation begins!

Metamorphosis of a caterpillar into a butterfly

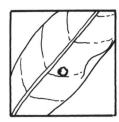 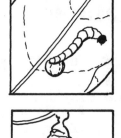  

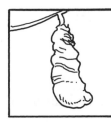 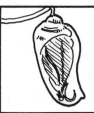 

What happens inside the cocoon or chrysalis?

During pupation, all of the caterpillar's body is broken down, and an adult body is formed from these "ingredients." The larva's little legs and antennae grow longer. It develops a curled tongue. Most remarkably, four wings are added! In some chrysalises, such as the monarch butterfly's, you can see the outline of the forming wings.

When and how does the butterfly or moth get out of the cocoon or chrysalis?

Pupae that have been formed during the spring or early summer hatch within a few weeks. At that time, the pupal case cracks open, and out crawls a wet and wrinkled adult moth or butterfly. The butterfly dries out its wings by pumping blood into them. The butterfly or moth climbs on a twig provided by nature (or you). It rests for an hour or so while its wings dry, and then flies away into the waiting sky. Be sure not to touch it while its wings are drying. And remember to release your butterfly or moth in a fairly secluded area so that it will not immediately fall prey to birds!

What are the caterpillar predators?

Birds eat them by the hundreds. Wasps, bats, toads, and small mammals such as shrews and skunks love the taste of the pupae.

How can caterpillars protect themselves?

Some caterpillars have great camouflage and hide from their enemies by blending in with leaves, dirt, or foliage. Others have stinging hairs or taste simply horrid. For example, the monarch eats milkweed, which has poisons that make animals sick. Not too many critters go back for second helpings once they've tasted a monarch!

Caterpillar Investigations

INVESTIGATION 1

Picky Eaters

You will need:

3 or 4 jars with vented tops

a place with a variety of plants and trees, such as maple, oak, cherry, and apple

3 or 4 plastic bags with twist ties or catching jars

tree and caterpillar guidebooks

Ask:

Will caterpillars eat a variety of leaves?

Hypothesize:

Make a prediction about whether caterpillars will eat more than one kind of tree leaf or **host plant.**

Procedure:

1. In the spring or early summer, go to an area with several kinds of trees. Bring your guidebooks.
2. Search the tree leaves (top and underneath) for caterpillars. (You may get faster results with the Caterpillar

Roundup method—see Activity 2). Try another tree if you don't get any caterpillars from the first one. You can do this investigation with even just one caterpillar.

3. Place each caterpillar in a plastic bag with 2 or 3 of the leaves from the tree it was on. Blow some air into the bag before you tie it with the twist tie. This arrangement is fine if you will be going right home. If not, use a catching jar. Plastic, which doesn't break, is best.
4. In a separate plastic bag, collect 3 or 4 leaves from other trees that are not the same as the ones on which you found the caterpillars.
5. At home, place each caterpillar in a jar with a different kind of leaf. Cover the jars with a vented lid.
6. Use the guidebooks to identify the leaves and the caterpillars.
7. Observe the caterpillars for the next 2 to 3 hours. When you finish your investigation, return the caterpillars to the trees on which you found them.

Results:

Which leaves did the caterpillars eat? Could you identify both the caterpillars and the tree leaves? Did any of them eat leaves that were different from the ones on which they were found? Which caterpillars ate which leaves? If you used only one caterpillar for this investigation, did it eat different kinds of leaves?

Conclusions:

Some caterpillars, such as the Polyphemus moth caterpillar, prefer oak leaves but will eat other leaves as well. Did your caterpillars do likewise? Can you make any conclusions from your investigation based on which leaves the caterpillars were eating?

Think about it:

Some creatures will eat only one kind of food. The panda eats only bamboo, and the monarch caterpillar eats only milkweed. How do you think this affects their chances for survival?

Midnight Munchies?

You will need:

1 or more caterpillars of the same species

the caterpillars' food source

plastic jar or bag for catching

2 large jars and tops with small breathing holes (get an adult to make the holes)

2 large empty pill jars (get permission to use them)

tape

cotton balls

for monarchs only: a large vase or jar and soft mesh screening and string

Ask:

Do caterpillars stop eating at night or whenever there's less light?

Hypothesize:

Make a prediction about the day or night (and light or dark) eating habits of caterpillars.

Procedure:

1. Go on a caterpillar hunt. Don't forget to look under leaves as well as on top. You'll be most successful if you look in the mid to late summer.
2. Try to collect 2 of the same species in the bag or jar. Also collect 2 small branches of leaves (or 2 stalks of milkweed for monarchs). You can do this investigation with one caterpillar; just set up one habitat and follow the rest of the procedure.
3. At home, set up 2 large jar habitats. Fill the pill jars with water, but not to the very top. Tape the pill jars inside the large jars. Place a branch of leaves in each pill jar and cover with cotton balls (so the caterpillar won't fall in and drown).
4. If you have a monarch and milkweed, place the plant in a large jar or vase with water. Smaller caterpillars (2 inches [5 cm] or less) will not leave the milkweed. If the monarch is larger than 2 inches, cover the vase with soft mesh screening and fasten with string around the base of the vase, since a larger caterpillar may be ready to seek a place to spin its chrysalis.
5. Place the caterpillars in the jars, sprinkle the leaves with water, and cover the jars with the tops with holes in them. Put one jar in a well-lit room, but not in direct sunlight. Put the other in a dark closet. If you have only one caterpillar, you can simply move it back and forth between light and dark areas to observe its eating habits.
6. After a few hours, observe the caterpillars and leaves in both jars. Observe what has or hasn't been eaten. In addition, place both

jars in a dark room at night. Ask your parents to observe whether the caterpillars are eating before they go to bed.

7. If you can't provide food for the caterpillars frequently, return them to the place where you found them the next day.

Results:

Was the caterpillar in the bright room eating? What about the caterpillar in the closet? Did one or both caterpillars eat at night?

Conclusions:

What can you conclude about caterpillar eating habits from your investigation?

Think about it:

Do you think other caterpillar species would have different eating habits related to lightness, darkness, and time of day? Try to find other species with which to test your hypotheses. Were the caterpillars' eating habits affected only by lightness and darkness, or by night and day? Could it be that caterpillars have an internal clock that determines behaviors such as eating?

INVESTIGATION 3

Caterpillar Safari

Ask:

How do caterpillars protect themselves?

Hypothesize:

Make predictions about caterpillars' adaptations for protection as you search for and learn to identify them. If you can't hunt outside for caterpillars, you can do this investigation using caterpillar guidebooks.

Procedure:

1. Go on your caterpillar safari in late spring, summer, or early fall, in any area that has lots of trees and plants. Bring your materials with you in a backpack. (You can pick up the long stick along the way. See Activity 2 for the Caterpillar Roundup method of finding caterpillars.)

> **You will need:**
>
> a caterpillar habitat (your backyard, the park, a trail, forests)
>
> an old sheet
>
> a long stick
>
> a caterpillar category chart
>
> a caterpillar guidebook
>
> a magnifying glass
>
> insect repellent

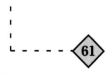

2. Look for caterpillars on the tops and undersides of leaves, on tree bark and branches, on plants and tall grasses, and on the ground. Use insect repellent in heavily wooded areas and watch out for ticks and poison ivy. Be able to identify these as well!

3. When you find a caterpillar, look at it closely with your magnifying glass. Locate its category on the category chart. Note its color and host plant. Use the guidebook to identify the species and other information about the caterpillar's adaptations for survival.

Caterpillar category chart

Smooth

Hairy

Spiney

Bumpy

Sluglike

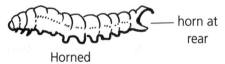
Bristly

Horned — horn at rear

Results:

Describe how you think each caterpillar can defend and protect itself. Does its color provide camouflage for blending into its surroundings? Does it have stinging hairs? How does the caterpillar's body shape, size, and parts help to protect it?

Conclusions:

Can you draw any conclusions about caterpillars' adaptations for survival from your observations and investigations?

Think about it:

Some caterpillars are brightly colored to warn predators that they are poisonous or bad-tasting. Can you think of other creatures whose coloration protects them in some way? (*Hint:* think about reptiles and amphibians.)

Caterpillar Activities

ACTIVITY 1

Pupae Search

Follow some simple steps to find a butterfly chrysalis or moth cocoon. You will need to be an excellent observer and nature detective for this activity.

Procedure:

1. You can search for chrysalises or cocoons in any area that has trees, bushes, and piles of leaves. They are hard to find because they are generally very well camouflaged.
2. If you are lucky enough to find one, make notes about where you found it. Draw a picture, noting whether the pupa or cocoon blended in with its surroundings.
3. If you found the pupa or cocoon near your home, you can observe its development day by day. If not, you may remove it only if this can be done without damaging it. Moth cocoons are usually on the ground; when you find one, place it in a jar with the soil and plant material where it was found. Remove a chrysalis only if it's suspended from a twig or object that you can

You will need:

a plastic container

a notebook and pencil

a caterpillar/butterfly guidebook

easily remove. A chrysalis is very fragile and will not travel well if it takes a long time to reach home. Its attachment, however, is usually very strong and can even withstand windy storms. Place the chrysalis and its twig in a large jar with a top (nylon, mesh, cheesecloth) fastened with an elastic band.

4. Check your cocoon or chrysalis often. When the metamorphosed creature emerges, check the guidebook to identify the species. You might want to draw a picture of the butterfly or moth.

5. Take the jar outside and remove the lid. Before long your moth or butterfly will fly away. What a wonder!

Lucky Caterpillar Roundup

ACTIVITY
2

With this simple activity you can round up several caterpillars in trees (and some other interesting little creatures, too!)

You will need:

one or more trees

an old white sheet
   (get an adult's
   permission to use it)

a long stick

a magnifying glass

caterpillar and other
   insect guidebooks

Procedure:

1. Place the sheet under a tree branch (one you can easily reach).
2. With a long stick, hit the base of the branch sharply. Be very careful not to hurt the tree!
3. If you're lucky, some tiny creatures will fall onto the sheet. If not, try your luck with another tree.
4. Once you've shaken down some caterpillars, look in your guidebook to identify the species. If you found other creatures, don't miss the opportunity to find out what they are by using the insect guidebook.
5. Observe your discoveries with a magnifying glass or take home a few critters and make a jar habitat. Don't forget to provide your visitors with leaves from the tree on which you found them.

Caterpillar Metamorphosis

ACTIVITY
3

From what you have learned about the life cycle of the butterfly, arrange these pictures in the correct order and write a description of what's happening in each picture.

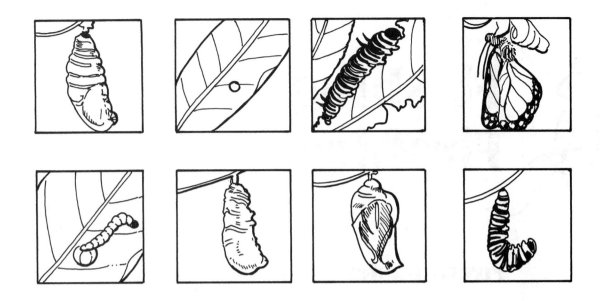

Procedure:

1. On the tracing paper, copy the illustrations in each square (or even better, draw them yourself). Color each square with crayons. (Markers may tear the tracing paper.)
2. Carefully cut out the tracing paper squares.
3. Arrange each square in the correct life-cycle order. If you're not sure, reread this chapter to check out which event occurred first, second, and so on.
4. Glue the squares onto the construction paper.
5. Can you describe what's happening in each picture? Either label each event with a short description or write a more detailed account of butterfly transformation. It also might be fun to write a story about a caterpillar's adventures on its way to becoming a butterfly. While the story would be fiction, the facts in the story would be real.

You will need:

a piece of tracing paper

2 pieces of construction or other heavy paper

a pencil

crayons

scissors

a ruler

a glue stick

6 Flashing Fireflies

Firefly Basics

Have you ever been out on a warm summer night and witnessed the magic of fireflies? When I was a child, my aunt told me that fireflies were specks of stars fallen from the heavens. Although I eventually learned the truth about fireflies, I still preferred to think of them as somewhat magical.

Fireflies, sometimes called lightning bugs, are not really flies at all. They are actually members of the beetle family **Lampyridae,** and they are distantly related to ladybugs. Isn't it fitting that the firefly's scientific name has the word "lamp" in it?

There are more than 1,900 species of fireflies worldwide, and more than 170 species in the United States. They are found on every continent except Antarctica. Each firefly species is different and prefers certain habitats. One of the most common fireflies of North America is *Photinus pyralis*. We'll find out more about this species later in the chapter.

People have been watching and collecting fireflies for thousands of years. A Chinese glossary that was written between 400 and 100 BC, identified the firefly as a winged insect with fire in its belly. Writers from ancient Greece, Rome, and India also mentioned them. There have been many superstitions and legends about fireflies. Modern scientists have tried to separate fact from fiction, but this hasn't always been easy. In some countries, people thought the firefly had special or magical powers. Long ago, the

Italian people believed that fireflies were the spirits of their dead ancestors. They were not always happy to see them flashing outside their homes at night! One old Japanese legend said that fireflies were the ghosts of brave warriors who gave up their lives for their country. Fireflies have always inspired people's imaginations in history, story, science, and even art.

Firefly collecting began in Japan long ago and is still a traditional summer pastime. Children hunt for them and put them in cages covered with cheesecloth, a light mesh-like material. Are you ready to capture lightning in a jar? Learning about the firefly will surely "spark" your imagination, too. While you're watching them on a summer night, also look for real shooting stars!

Where can I find them?

As you have learned, different firefly species prefer different habitats. You might find them in forests and fields or right in your own backyard in the grass and around bushes and shrubs. Begin looking in the spring and summer at twilight, when it first gets dark. Reduce any extra lighting where you're looking, since this light will interfere with the firefly's signals. You will also be able to see them better in the dark.

How can I catch them?

Fireflies

Bring a plastic catching container with you on your firefly search. Ask an adult to poke air holes in the lid. One easy way to catch a firefly is to watch the flashing blink, then try to determine where the next blink will be. Try to attract fireflies with a small flashlight (see Activity 1). Spot a flying firefly, wait two seconds (say "one Mississippi, two Mississippi") after it flashes, then flash your light for half a second. Did you find a flashing firefly friend?

How can I keep them?

If you want to keep the fireflies overnight (one night only, or they may not live), keep them in a glass or plastic jar. Add a damp paper towel or cotton balls to supply moisture and grass and a few twigs for them to perch on. Cover the container with nylon or mesh fastened with an elastic band. If you keep your fireflies in your bedroom, you can pretend their sparkles are tiny bits of fallen stars!

There's no need to feed them, since adult fireflies almost never eat. Read on to find out why. Release your visitors the next morning so that they can light up another night sky.

Firefly Observations

After observing your fireflies, you will probably have many questions about them. This tiny creature's **anatomy** (inside and outside body parts) and behaviors can be very complicated, so you'll have to be

External

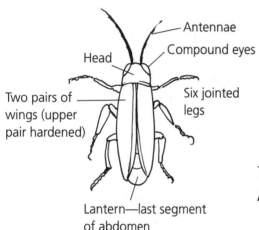

- Antennae
- Compound eyes
- Head
- Two pairs of wings (upper pair hardened)
- Six jointed legs
- Lantern—last segment of abdomen

Internal

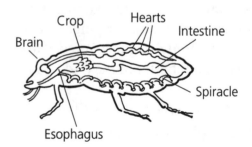

- Brain
- Crop
- Hearts
- Intestine
- Spiracle
- Esophagus

The anatomy of the firefly. Look for these body parts:

Antennae: Feelers, which help the firefly sense his surroundings.

Elytra: The first pair of wings, which have a protective covering and are used for balance in flight.

Lantern: The flashing part of the abdomen.

scientifically alert! After all the explaining is done, you will be even more fascinated by these lovely, complex creatures!

Find out More about Fireflies

How does a firefly's light work?

Get ready for some technical language here! The firefly's light comes from a chemical reaction that takes place in special cells in its body called **photocytes.** The photocytes have two chemicals, **luciferin** and **luciferase.** These chemicals are needed to make light. When the firefly pushes oxygen into the photocytes, the oxygen, luciferin, and luciferase all combine with other chemicals. The complex process that takes place gives off energy in the form of light. This process is called **bioluminescence** because light (luminescence) is produced by a biological process. (**Biology** is the study of living things.)

Do other living creatures produce bioluminescence?

Yes. Many fish and other sea creatures produce bioluminescence. Also, many other insects (mostly beetles), such as the railroad worm and ground and click beetles, can produce light.

Why do fireflies flash their lights?

There are a few reasons why fireflies flash. One reason is that the flashes are part of a signal system for attracting mates. Another reason is that the light tells birds and other insects that the firefly is not a good meal. The chemicals in the lantern of the firefly are bitter-tasting. (Do you think someone tasted one to find out?) However, this does not keep some other critters, such as frogs, from eating huge numbers of them! Also, scientists think fireflies use distress flashing to warn other fireflies of danger. If a firefly is caught in a spider web, it will flash rapidly.

Does the firefly's light feel hot?

No. The chemical reaction produces no heat, so it is called cold light. Some species of fireflies flash more in hot weather, but the flash is still cold light.

How do male and female fireflies flash to one another?

Each species of firefly has its own special light signal, and scientists have been able to decode about 130 of them. A female usually waits in the grass. When she sees the signal of her species, she responds by flashing her own light. The female waits for a certain amount of time before responding. Her answering flash tells the male that she is a potential partner. When these two meet, they mate. You can recognize the common *Photinus Pyralis* firefly because it always rises upward as it flashes.

When do fireflies begin flashing?

This depends on the species, but most begin flashing at different times after sunset. In the United States, flashing occurs most often on moonless nights when the temperature is above 80 degrees Fahrenheit (26°C). They also flash more when the summer follows a damp spring. Why do you think fireflies are great flashers in the tropics?

Do fireflies sleep?

Yes. Around nine o'clock in the evening the fireflies' glow fades, and they go to sleep.

How and where do female fireflies lay their eggs?

After mating, the female crawls under a leaf. The eggs come out of an **ovipositor,** a small tube at the back of the abdomen of her body. She may lay 500 or more eggs, depending on the species. Some species lay their eggs on moss or grass. Each egg is about the size of a period on this page! After about 30 days, the eggs become strange-looking little creatures with wormlike bodies.

How does a baby firefly grow?

Like many other insects, the firefly develops through the growth process known as metamorphosis. As soon as it hatches from the egg, the young insect or larva begins looking for food. It searches for snails, little worms, and the larva of other insects. As it grows, it molts (sheds its skin) several times so it can expand. It looks a little different each time it sheds. The larva can also produce light. When fall comes, the larva burrows into the ground or crawls under a rock and rests for the winter. In the spring, it comes out and eats for a few weeks. Then it burrows into the ground where, in about 5 weeks, it molts for the last time. This next stage is the pupa. The pupa begins to grow wings and make other changes. In about 10 days, it reaches the fourth and last stage of its life as an adult firefly.

What does the adult firefly eat?

Most adult fireflies don't eat at all! They live on the nourishment they stored as larvae. They do take moisture from dew and plant leaves. Their adult lives are very short. Females die within four weeks of laying their eggs, and the males die soon after mating. Only one adult firefly is an exception to the "no eating" rule. The *Photuris* species feeds on other fireflies. It imitates the response message of the female of another species and lures a flashing male. Then it gobbles him up! That particular male will have lived an even shorter than usual life!

What are the firefly predators?

Birds, fish, frogs, and toads eat firefly larvae. With the exception of *Photuris,* the adult firefly is rarely another creature's prey.

Firefly Investigations

Firefly Communication

Ask:

How do different species of fireflies communicate with flash signals?

Hypothesize:

You have learned that fireflies' flashes have patterns, depending upon the species. The signals might vary in several ways, such as the duration of the flashes, the color, the time between signals, and the number of flashes in a signal. How do you think members of different species find others of their species to mate with? Make a prediction about this.

Procedure:

1. Before you begin, make two charts to record your observations (one for each site):

	Number of Flashes in a Signal	Color	Time Between Signals
SITE 1:			
Male 1			
Male 2			
Male 3			
Male 4			
SITE 2:			
Male 1			
Male 2			
Male 3			
Male 4			

> **You will need:**
>
> newspaper
>
> 2 different places to observe fireflies, such as a backyard, the woods, a field, even in the city
>
> a pencil
>
> a notebook
>
> a stopwatch or a watch with a second hand

2. Look in the newspaper to find out when sunset will occur on the day of your first observation.
3. Begin your observations at your first site about 30 minutes before sunset. Watch for flashing males and record the number of flashes in a signal, the color, and time between signals. Follow some of the males to see whether they locate females.
4. Follow the same procedure at your second observation site. Record your results even if you can find only one species at both sites.

Results:

Did the signals differ at the two locations? What were your signal results for either one or two species? Did any of the males locate a female?

Conclusions:

Could you make any conclusions about how different species communicate? If you observed the same species rather than different ones, what could you conclude about the male's flashing patterns? If you observed two or more species, how did the signals differ? Did you see the colors of the males' flashes at different times of the evening?

Think about it:

If you observed different-colored flashes, you saw different firefly species. Fireflies with mostly yellow colors are usually seen at twilight (the beginning of sunset). As it gets darker, fireflies with darker, greenish hues begin flashing. Why do you think this occurs?

INVESTIGATION 2

Fireflies and Temperature

Ask:

How do fireflies respond to changes in temperature?

Hypothesize:

From what you have learned about fireflies, make a prediction about whether they will flash more frequently in warmer or colder temperatures.

Procedure:

1. Make a chart like the one below to record the fireflies' signals:

<table>
<tr><td></td><td>Firefly's Flashes per Minute</td></tr>
<tr><td>In jar not in water</td><td></td></tr>
<tr><td>In jar in warm water</td><td></td></tr>
<tr><td>In jar in iced water</td><td></td></tr>
</table>

You will need:

a jar with one or more fireflies

a pot or other container with lukewarm water

a pot or container with iced water

a stopwatch or a watch or clock with a second hand

paper and pencil

2. First, observe the fireflies in your jar when it is not in water and note how many flashes occur per minute.
3. Place the jar in the pot of lukewarm water. Be sure the water is not hot. Record the number of flashes per minute. Take the jar out of the water and let it return to room temperature. This will take a few minutes.
4. Next, place the jar in iced water. If your jar is too warm, it will crack when placed in cold water, so be very careful! Again, record the number of flashes per minute. Remove the jar quickly so your fireflies will not be affected by the cold.

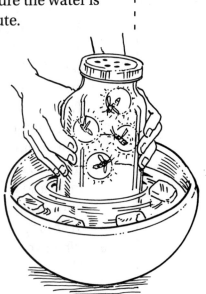

Results:

Did the fireflies flash more frequently when the jar temperature was warmer or colder? Did their flashes give less light in hot or cold conditions?

Conclusions:

A firefly's flashing is affected by air temperature. The higher the temperature, the more frequent the flashes and the brighter they are. Did your investigation support this?

Think about it:

During what other circumstances might the fireflies' flashes increase in duration? Why? In what ways does this ability to respond to change protect the firefly?

Love at First Flash?

You will need:

male and female fireflies

a small plastic catching jar

a 5- or 10-gallon (19 or 38-liter) aquarium or large jar with a vented lid

your backyard or a place with long grass

the flashing diagram (figure 6.5)

Ask:

Will captive female and male fireflies signal and respond to one another?

Hypothesize:

Make a prediction about fireflies' behavior in captivity.

Procedure:

1. Read Activity 1 to learn ways to attract fireflies.
2. Before you begin your search, place a few long stems of grass in the aquarium or jar. An aquarium is best since the fireflies will have more room in it to fly and signal.
3. At dusk you will need to be in a place that has long grass. Remember, the male fireflies will be flying and moving during each flash; the females sit on tall grass stems and watch the males. Therefore, search both in the air and on the ground.
4. Try to capture 1 or 2 females and 1 or 2 males, and transfer them to the larger container in the house. (You may have to make more than one searching trip.)
5. In a darkened room, observe and study the differences between male and female signals. The male flashes, and then, a few seconds later, the female responds. Most female signals are a series of short pulses of about the same degree of brightness.
6. When you observe an exchange of signals, make a diagram to illustrate the flashing patterns.

Results:

Did your captive fireflies flash to one another? Could you observe the differences between the male and female signals? How? Could you tell which two fireflies were signaling to one another?

Conclusions:

If you were able to determine whether fireflies respond to one another in captivity, you can draw some conclusions from this investigation. If not, do you need more trials with other fireflies to find out?

Think about it:

How does the male know whether the female flashing is his species? Do you remember why he would want to avoid the female Photuris species? (Hint: It's a matter of life or death!) If your fireflies didn't signal to one another in captivity, why do you think this was so?

Firefly flashing patterns

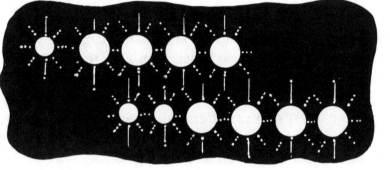

Male

Female

Firefly Activities

Become a Female Flasher
(for both boys and girls!)

In this activity, you will send flashing signals like a female firefly and try to attract a male!

It's important to know more about the signals you'll be flashing. As we learned, one of the most common fireflies in eastern North America is *Photinus pyralis*. *Photinus* flies in an up-and-down pattern and flashes its bright, yellow light only when it's rising. At sundown, it flashes J-shaped signals near the ground. Later in the evening it flies higher, but with the same J-shaped signal.

The flash code of *Photinus* is easy to follow. The flying male flashes a series about 6 seconds apart. The female, down in the

A male firefly's
J-shaped signal

grass, flashes her response about 2 seconds later. While the male flies toward the female, they both continue this sequence until they meet.

Now, here's where you come in! You can play the role of the female flasher and lure a male firefly to you! All you need is a small flashlight and a place where you see the J-shaped flashes of a *Photinus*.

Procedure:

1. Hold the flashlight close to the ground.
2. When you see the male's J-shaped flash, count two seconds ("one Mississippi, two Mississippi . . ."), then turn on the flashlight for one second. The male should start heading toward your light. If he flashes again, wait two seconds and flash again. Continue this response pattern until he approaches you. He might even land right on your hand!
3. Release him so he can find a real mate!

ACTIVITY
2

Glow-in-the-Dark Critter

Even if you can't find live fireflies, you can make a glowing beetle.

Procedure:

1. Glue 3 cotton balls in a row to represent the head, thorax, and abdomen of the firefly.
2. Cut out a pair of wings from the construction paper and glue them to the thorax.
3. Make black dots for eyes on the head (compound eyes, of course!)
4. Dip 2 small pieces of pipe cleaner into glue and stick them into the head for antennae.
5. Paint the abdomen (the third cotton ball) with glow-in-the-dark paint.
6. When the paint dries, dim the lights and imagine that your flasher friend is alive! And you don't have to release this one!

A Magical Story About a Firefly

In this activity, you can create your own firefly hero!
You might gather some friends or classmates together and tell them
your story, or you could write it down.

Many legends about fireflies have been passed down through the
ages. As you learned in the beginning of this chapter, some people
long ago thought that fireflies were the spirits of their dead ancestors or the ghosts of warriors killed in battle. It was also recorded
that people in China and Japan kept fireflies in cages to provide
light. Legend has it that Ch'e Yin, a Chinese scholar who died in A.D.
399, was too poor to afford lamp oil, so he studied at night by the
light of caged fireflies!

You can tell a story that might have taken place hundreds of years
ago, or you can let your imagination run wild with tales of astound-
ing fireflies in the present or future. Perhaps you caught just one
special firefly and kept it for your own. Your amazing insect might
have super-firefly powers, charged by its amazing flash! What can
your firefly do?

PART

II

Attracting Wildlife to Your Backyard

7 Bird Feeding and Housing

Have you ever heard the saying "She eats like a bird"? People who often say this are referring to someone who doesn't eat very much, but what many people don't know is that birds eat quite a bit. Even the smallest are always on the lookout for food. Flying, nest building, and keeping warm in winter are activities that burn up lots of calories.

Feeding birds is popular in many areas. Whether you are interested in feeding pigeons and ducks in your neighborhood park or using a fancy feeder in your backyard, this chapter will help get you started. Let's consider some commonly asked questions about feeding birds and about birdfeeders.

What should I feed the birds?

This depends on what kinds (species) of birds you wish to attract. You may simply want to feed the birds that you already see in your yard or neighborhood, or you may want to try to attract ones that are not so common. You might want to do both! You can experiment with different kinds of food (and feeders) to see which kinds attract the best variety or the most birds. As your bird identification skills improve, you may have favorites that you'll especially want to feed. The seed mixes sold in grocery and department stores contain seeds that are not necessarily the favorites of birds. Two types of seed are the most recommended for backyard feeders: black-oil sunflower and white proso millet. The sunflower seeds (mostly for hopper-style feeders) attract the widest variety of species, and millet is a favorite of ground feeding species like doves, juncos, and towhees.

Other seeds that birds like are striped and hulled sunflower, cracked and fine corn and thistle (niger), which is a favorite of finches and many other songbirds.

Orioles, tanagers, mockingbirds, and many other birds love fruit such as apples, oranges, bananas, and raisins. Place these on a plat-form or window-sill feeder, or make a nice fruit pizza! (See Activity 6).

Suet, which is a type of beef fat, is a special favorite of birds in the winter. Suet gives them energy, which they need to stay warm during the long, cold months. You can find suet in the supermarket or butcher shop. Many birds, will come to your suet feeder, including insect-eating birds such as woodpeckers, kinglets, creepers, wrens and thrashers. You can tell they are just loving every bite!

Experiment with your bird feeding! Try out some of the special recipes in this chapter and make up your own. The birds will surely appreciate all your generous offerings.

What kind of feeders should I use?

Birdfeeders come in many shapes and sizes. Store-bought feeders can be simple and inexpensive or more elaborate and costly. You might have more fun (and save money) by making your own feeders. Several birdfeeder activities are included in this chapter.

Some feeders can be placed on a pole or hung from a wire or a tree branch. For those of you who don't have a backyard, there are bird-feeders that can be attached directly to a window.

If you'd like to attract a wide variety of birds, consider having a feeding station. This could include:

- ◆ a hanging feeder
- ◆ a ground or platform feeder
- ◆ a window feeder
- ◆ a suet container
- ◆ a water source

A backyard feeding station

Hanging or Hopper Feeders

One of the most popular feeders is the hopper type. Hopper feeders allow only a certain amount of seeds out at a time. Hoppers come in many shapes, including tubes, made of clear glass or plastic, and boxes, usually made of wood with a pane of glass or plastic on two sides. These feeders can be hung from a wire or mounted on a pole. You can customize your feeder by attaching one or two sticks to the feeder poles using string or wire. These will be extra perches where birds can sit while waiting their turn at the feeder. Hang fruit slices from these branches, and you may attract more kinds of birds. See the activities in this chapter to find out how to make your own hopper feeders.

Hopper feeders

Platform
feeders

Ground or Platform Feeders

Ground or platform feeders attract birds such as bluejays, brown-headed cowbirds, cardinals, common grackles, crows, juncos, mourning doves, bob-whites, pigeons, red-winged black-birds, pheasants, towhees, sparrows, and many other species, depending on where you live. Ground feeders also usually attract a lot of squirrels and chipmunks, not to mention mice and rats that may come to dine at night! Keep your ground feeders farther from your house than the other feeders so you won't encourage the mice to visit you indoors! Platform feeders are easy to make (with an adult's help).

Window Feeders

You can buy small feeders that suction to your window. These are great fun because they allow you to see the birds up close from inside your house. Window box feeders are excellent since they are large and can be cleaned from inside your house. They fit snugly right into the open window so the outside air can't come in. Window box feeders can be expensive, but they are one of the best ways to watch bird behavior. It takes a while for birds to come to these feeders and to become accustomed to humans peering at them. Keep at a distance at first. Before long they'll accept you as part of the scenery!

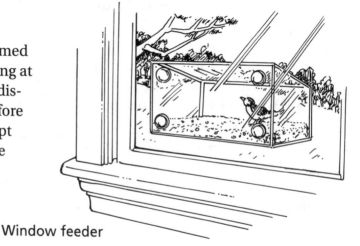

Window feeder

Suet Feeders

As we said, suet is a big favorite of birds in winter. See Activity 3, "Sensational Suet Feeders" for what to buy and make to help keep your feathered friends warm. You can also buy suet feeders and premixed blocks of suet and seed mixtures.

Birdfeeder Maintenance

When shopping for any kind of feeder, think about how durable it will be. Will it keep the seeds dry? Is it easy to clean? Which species will use it? As you learn more about birds and observe them, you can make decisions about which birds you'd like to attract. Whatever feeders you choose, be sure to keep them clean, for the health of your feathered friends.

Suet
feeder

Water

Birds need water year-round, especially in winter when their usual water sources may be frozen. A bird bath can serve this purpose. You're probably familiar with the cement ones, which can be expensive. If your parents agree to buy one, be sure it's one that sits on a pedestal. Ground baths are an invitation to bird predators, like cats! You can also easily make your own water sources for birds, as we described in the activity section of this chapter. The water level of any bird baths should be no deeper than 3 inches (8 cm).

Bird bath

A Note about Nest Boxes and Birdhouses

Nest boxes, in various shapes and sizes, can be provided for cavity-dwelling birds such as woodpeckers, flickers, wrens, swallows, chickadees, titmice, nuthatches, kestrels, screech owls, and bluebirds. A nest box is a covered wooden box with an entry hole. The size of both the box and the hole depend on the species of bird you want to attract.

Some birds use birdhouses for shelter and not necessarily to raise young. Most birdhouses are made of wood. If you want to buy a nest box or birdhouse, visit your local bird-watcher store. You and your family can also make nest boxes and shelters for your backyard birds. Shelf-type houses are the easiest to make. The most elaborate are purple martin houses, which have three or more stories! Building a birdhouse is a great way to learn some basic carpentry and to share some fun time with a favorite grown-up.

Nest boxes and birdhouses

Will squirrels be a problem?

As you will soon discover, birds may not be the only visitors to your feeder! Squirrels and chipmunks love seeds, too, and need food surpluses in the winter. It can be a challenge to keep these rodents from emptying your feeder long before the birds do! They may even destroy wooden or plastic feeders. Try to solve potential squirrel problems before they begin by discussing this with a bird-store salesperson, nature center staff, or other experienced folks who feed birds. Some will surely tell you that squirrels are so clever that not much can prevent them from reaching your feeder, but other folks have had some success. Find those folks!

Try to locate your feeders at least 10 feet (3 meters) away from trees, rooftops, and other structures, since squirrels can jump amazing distances onto your feeder. They are also fearless and don't seem to mind falling from great heights.

You can buy "squirrel baffles," which fit many types of feeders. There are even expensive feeders that close down when a squirrel or heavy bird steps onto the feeding tray! However, the clever varmint in my backyard simply leaned around the side while lifting the feeding bar with his hand.

Another possible solution for pole feeders is to place a wide, galvanized stove pipe around the pole. Even agile squirrels can't climb up this! For the time being, this is working for me, though it probably won't be long before the clever ones find a solution!

Cats, not squirrels, are actually the real threat to backyard birds. Birds will avoid feeding areas where a cat stalks them. Ask your neighbors who have free-roaming cats to equip them with a bell-collar to warn birds of their approach.

How can I identify birds?

Birds are identified by their size, shape, color, markings, flight, behavior, song, and habitat (where they live). There are many excellent field guides to help you, and some are written especially for young people. Field guides have pictures of hundreds of birds and short descriptions of their habits. They discuss **field marks** (details about a bird's appearance) and sometimes have range maps that show where each species lives. Check the information you've gathered about your bird against the information in the field guide. Bird identification can be difficult since many birds of the same species look similar to one another. You may even spot a bird that is out of its normal range. (If you do, call your local nature center or bird sanctuary, since they collect information like this.) The more often and more closely you observe birds, the better you will get at bird identification. In time you will be able to call yourself a "birder," the name given to serious bird-watchers!

It's great fun to keep track of each new bird you identify. Get a notebook and write down the names of the birds you see, a description of their appearance and behavior, and the date you saw them. Draw a sketch, if you'd like. You can also buy printed field cards that list the names of birds and have a space where you can check off the birds you see. Most birders have a "life list" to help them keep track of every bird they see. You'll find these inexpensive lists in bird supply stores.

Before long, you'll want to know more about the birds on your list. You may be able to identify pigeons, but what do you know about them? What sounds do they make? How can you tell a male from a female? How many eggs does a pigeon lay? What does a baby pigeon look like? And that question asked by so many people, "Has anyone ever actually *seen* a baby pigeon?!" You can find out some answers to your bird questions by observing them closely. Write down what you see in a notebook. For questions you can't answer by observing, do some research in books or on the Internet. Birds are *cool!*

Activities for the Birds!

Make a Milk Carton Birdfeeder

ACTIVITY
1

This is a nice, temporary feeder that should last at least a few months.

You will need:

a half-gallon cardboard milk carton

a ruler

a pen

scissors

a hole punch

twine

birdseed or suet

Procedure:

1. Measure and mark a line 2½ inches (6.25 cm) down from the top edge of the carton on two adjoining sides.
2. Measure and mark a line 2½ inches (6.25 cm) up from the bottom of the carton on the same two sides.
3. Cut the sides off between the marked lines on the two adjoining sides.
4. Using a small hole punch, make two small holes in the very top edge of the carton.
5. Put twine through the holes.
6. Fill the feeder with seeds or suet and hang from a branch or pole.

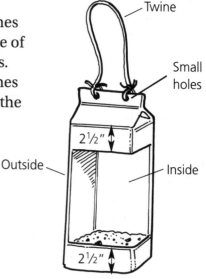

Milk carton feeder

Make a Detergent Bottle Feeder

This one is easy to make, and a good way to recycle plastic!

Procedure:

1. Trace the outline of the rim of a glass or the lid of a mustard jar (or something approximately that size) on opposite sides of the detergent bottle. Those circles should be about 4 inches (10 cm) from the bottom of the bottle.

2. Cut the holes out with scissors. This can be especially hard to get started, so you may need adult help.

3. Use a hole punch (if the bottle isn't too thick), or have an adult use a nail or a drill (if it's *really* thick!), to make two holes, right under the circles, for a perch.

4. Insert the dowel or stick all the way through the perch holes. Allow about 3 inches (8 cm) on each side of the bottle for the birds to perch on.

5. Punch or have an adult drill small holes in the bottom of the bottle so that rainwater will drain out.

6. Fill the bottle with seed and wrap and tie the twine tightly around the bottle cap. Hang away from places where squirrels can reach it.

Put feed in here

Perch

Detergent bottle feeder

> **You will need:**
>
> a detergent bottle rinsed out very well
>
> scissors
>
> a glass or mustard jar lid
>
> a hole punch or thick nail
>
> a drill (optional, for adult use only)
>
> one 10–12 inch (25–30 cm) dowel or stick (depending on the width of the base of the bottle)
>
> a marker
>
> twine

ACTIVITY
3

Make Sensational Suet Feeders

Suet is available in the meat section of grocery stores. Remember to provide it for the birds only in winter, since heat will cause suet to spoil quickly. Keep suet far from the reach of other animals like squirrels and raccoons, who will gladly take the whole thing! You can buy metal or plastic suet feeders, but the safest and easiest ones for the birds are the ones you can make.

Mesh Bag Suet Feeder

Fill a mesh onion bag with suet. Before putting it in the bag, you can roll the suet in seeds for an extra treat. The seeds also help the birds get at the fat. Hang the bag from a tree using rope, twine, or a wire coat hanger.

Mesh bag suet feeder

Log Suet Feeder

You will need:

a thick branch or piece of log

a drill

a large eye-hook

small dowels (optional)

a sturdy rope or chain

adult help

Procedure:

1. Find a thick branch (with shorter branches attached) or a small log that is not rotting. Cut the shorter branches back to about 3 inches (5 cm).
2. Ask an adult to drill or carve 1-inch (2.5-cm) holes above the branches (or in the log).
3. If you are using a log and wish to have perches, ask the adult to drill small holes just below the larger holes and insert small dowels into the holes.
4. Fill the larger holes with suet (or peanut butter).
5. Screw in the eye-hook and hang the feeder pole where squirrels can't reach.

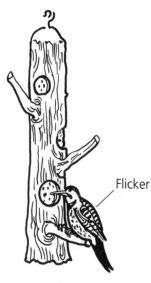

Flicker

Log suet feeder

ACTIVITY
4

Make a Tray Platform Feeder

Have an adult drill drainage holes in a large, flat piece of wood. Place gravel or sand on top of the wood to provide more drainage. Spread cracked corn and seeds on top (or other suggested ground feeder foods). The platform can be placed directly on the ground, perched on a tree stump, or suspended by rope from a low branch, attached by eye-hooks at each corner of the wood. An adult can also build a rim around the platform feeder. Clean up bird droppings and seed shells often. You may get other diners, too, so be ready to share. Shoo away unwanted guests when you're around!

Make Christmas Tree and Pine Cone Feeders

You can recycle your Christmas tree for bird use! Stand your tree in your backyard after you and your family have removed all the lights and ornaments. String popcorn, stale doughnuts and cranberries or other fresh or dried fruit, and drape the strings around the tree. Tie on some small mesh suet bags. What a perfect way to extend the holidays for your feathered friends! You can also slather a large pine cone with peanut butter and roll it in seeds. (Save the jelly for your own sandwich!) The seeds will make the peanut butter easier for the birds to eat since they don't have saliva. With string, tie the cone to your recycled Christmas tree or another tree.

Christmas Tree Feeder

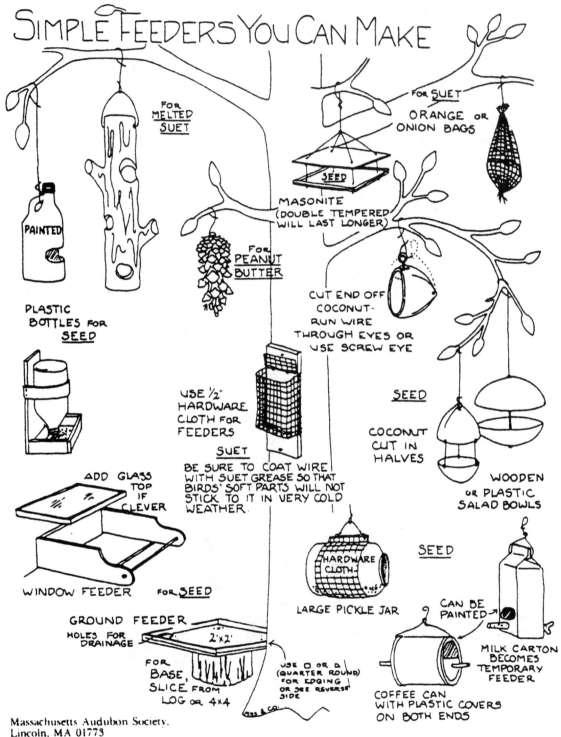

SIMPLE FEEDERS YOU CAN MAKE

FOR MELTED SUET

PAINTED

PLASTIC BOTTLES FOR SEED

FOR PEANUT BUTTER

FOR SUET
ORANGE OR ONION BAGS

SEED

MASONITE (DOUBLE TEMPERED WILL LAST LONGER)

CUT END OFF COCONUT- RUN WIRE THROUGH EYES OR USE SCREW EYE

SEED

COCONUT CUT IN HALVES

WOODEN OR PLASTIC SALAD BOWLS

USE ½" HARDWARE CLOTH FOR FEEDERS

SUET
BE SURE TO COAT WIRE WITH SUET GREASE SO THAT BIRDS' SOFT PARTS WILL NOT STICK TO IT IN VERY COLD WEATHER.

ADD GLASS TOP IF CLEVER

WINDOW FEEDER

FOR SEED

HARDWARE CLOTH

LARGE PICKLE JAR

SEED

CAN BE PAINTED

MILK CARTON BECOMES TEMPORARY FEEDER

GROUND FEEDER
HOLES FOR DRAINAGE

2'x2'

FOR BASE, SLICE FROM LOG OR 4x4

USE □ OR □ (QUARTER ROUND) FOR EDGING OR SEE REVERSE SIDE

COFFEE CAN WITH PLASTIC COVERS ON BOTH ENDS

Massachusetts Audubon Society.
Lincoln. MA 01773

Be a Chef for the Birds

Prepare these simple recipes and watch your feathered friends flock to your yard at mealtime!

Cornbread Supreme

Directions:

Mix all the ingredients together. Have an adult help you bake according to the package directions. When the bread has cooled, cut it into squares and crumble it onto a platform feeder or the ground. Freeze any extra bread for another day. The birds will gobble this up. (Shoo, squirrels, you can't eat it all!)

Equipment:

square baking pan

mixing bowl

mixing spoon

oven

Ingredients:

cornbread mix

2 eggs (add shells from one egg)

1 cup (227 g) birdseed mix

Bountiful Bird Bread

(*Note:* The amount of ingredients depends on the size of the bread and on how much you want to fill it.)

Directions:

Cut off one end of the bread and hollow out the loaf. (You can crumble up the insides and feed this bread to the birds.) Leave ½ inch (40 mm) of bread on the loaf bottom. Mix together all of the ingredients except the graham crackers, and fill the loaf with this mixture. Stand the crackers on top. (The birds can perch on the crackers as they eat the mixture and will also love to eat the crackers!) Push the post or long stick several inches into the ground and gently push the bread onto it (vertically).

Equipment:

knife

mixing bowl

mixing spoon

Ingredients:

round loaf of 1- or 2-day-old bread (whole, not sliced)

rope, twine, or yarn

1 cup (227 g) peanut butter

¼ cup (57 g) each: cornmeal, raisins, peanuts, sunflower seeds

2 or 3 graham crackers

post or long, thick stick

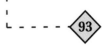

Equipment:

pizza pan or baking pan

heavy pan

mixing bowl

mixing spoon

pizza cutter or knife

Ingredients:

2 pounds (.9 kg) suet

1 cup (57 g) peanut butter
   (chunky is great)

¼ cup (57 g) each: raisins, seeds,
   wheat germ, chopped fruit,
   chopped nuts

½ cup (113 g) each: bread
   crumbs, oatmeal, cornmeal

flour if needed

Pizza Bird-Style (Hold the Pepperoni!)

Feel free to improvise on these ingredients! If *you* were a bird, what would you like on your pizza?

Directions:

Have an adult help you melt the suet and peanut butter over low heat in a heavy pan. Mix the rest of the ingredients in a large bowl. Add the suet/peanut butter mix, gradually stirring. If it's not thick enough, add flour or extra bread crumbs, oatmeal, or cornmeal. Spread this mixture on a greased pizza pan or baking sheet, freeze, and then cut with a pizza cutter or knife. You can place the pizza on a platform feeder or on the ground, away from the house.

(*Note:* You can also freeze these ingredients in a 9-by-5 (23-cm by 13-cm) breadpan, then cut into pieces later as needed. Line the pans with plastic wrap for easy removal.)

ACTIVITY 7

Crafty Bird Baths

If you don't want to purchase a bird bath, you can make your own. A bath can be as simple as a bowl holding a few inches of water or craftier ones such as those offered here. Whatever kind of bath you choose, be sure to keep it very clean and high enough off the ground to discourage bird predators. Also provide water sources for birds in winter since many natural sources are frozen.

You will need:

2 plastic planters or other types of bowls,
   one large, one smaller. The smaller bowl
   will nestle inside the larger one.

soil

small stones for soil drainage

grass seed and/or low-growing flowers
   such as pansies, clover, marigolds, etc.

Grassy Garden Bowl Bath

Procedure:

1. The smaller bowl will be the bird-bath pool and the larger one will contain the grass and/or flowers. Place small stones (for soil drainage) on the bottom of the larger bowl.

2. Fill the outer bowl with soil, allowing a few inches of space at the top. Nestle the smaller bowl in the middle of the larger one.

3. Sprinkle grass seed and/or plant flowers in the soil of the outer bowl. Plant grass seed as early as possible in the spring.

4. Fill the inside bowl with water. Before long, the grass will be growing and even before that, the birds will be splashing and drinking! Trim the grass with a scissors when it gets too long.

Hanging Pan Bath

Procedure:

1. Ask an adult to poke holes in the rim of the pie pan in 4 places equally distant from one another.

2. Fasten (by knotting) 4 lengths of twine or thin rope (about 1 foot or 30 cm) in each hold (as shown in diagram). Gather each length of twine and tie together at the top.

3. Hang from a tree with another piece of twine. Fill with a few inches of water. It may take a few days for the birds to discover their new pool, but it's so much fun to watch them when they do!

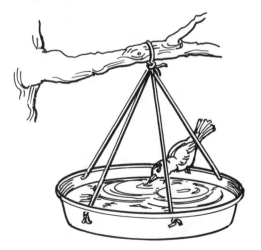

You will need:

an aluminum pie pan

tool for making holes in pan (for adult use only)

strong twine or thin rope

8 Hovering Hummingbirds

If ever a bird seemed magical, it is the hummingbird! It flashes its iridescent tiny self before you, then just as suddenly it's gone! People have always been enchanted by hummingbirds, and fortunately for them and for us, they are easy to attract to your backyard.

The hummingbird is the smallest member of the bird family. There are sixteen species of hummingbirds in the United States and about 338 species worldwide. If you live in the Southwest or on the West Coast of the United States, you may see 15 species of humming-birds, but if you live in the midwestern or eastern part of the country, you will see only one, the ruby-throated hummingbird. We'll focus on the ruby-throated, but you might want to learn more specifics about the species in your area.

You can identify the ruby-throated by its shiny green head, back, and tail. Only the male has the bright ruby throat. The females are not as flashy as the males, but they are very pretty in their own right. The ruby-throated

Hummingbirds

weighs from .09 to .14 of an ounce (2.5 to 4 g), about the weight of a penny! Look for ruby-throateds in May when their favorite flowers start to bloom.

Hummingbirds are amazing flyers. They can fly forward, backward, sideways, and even upside down! Their wings beat 78 times per second during regular flight and up to 200 times per second during a power dive. That's why their wings look blurry when they're hovering. They can hover because their wings are rigid, except at the shoulder joint. This allows the wings to move in all directions in a hovering figure-8 pattern. It is the wings rapidly pushing against the air that causes the humming noise that gives these "hummers" their name. They have to feed every 10 minutes or so all day long to keep up their energy.

Hummingbirds don't eat seeds like your other bird visitors. To attract them, you'll have to provide them with the food they like, such as nectar, which other bird species drink. Hummingbirds get nectar from flowers and tree sap. They also need protein to build their muscles, so they eat small spiders, gnats, aphids, and lots of tiny flies.

These tiny birds can be very aggressive! They will attack much larger birds such as crows and even hawks. They guard their territories fiercely against other hummingbirds and compete for nectar and insects. They use their bills and claws as weapons and may dive-bomb each other, colliding in midair. Whichever bird flies away is the loser, but they seldom are harmed by these fights. Their predators include hawks, crows, roadrunners, snakes, lizards, frogs, and some spiders. In the wild, they live from three to five years.

How can I attract hummingbirds to my backyard?

The best way to attract hummingbirds is to plant the flowers they love for nectar. See Activity 1 about hummingbird gardening. But you can also attract them with a feeder, which you can purchase in a bird supply store or make yourself (see Activity 2). The feeders are made to hold a nectar solution, and they come in many different shapes and sizes. Most have red parts, since hummingbirds love red. Choose a feeder that looks easy to clean, and ask a salesperson for advice about this. To prevent the solution from spoiling, buy a small feeder at first. Or simply buy a larger one and don't fill it up all the way. Most important, keep your feeders clean and wash them with very hot water, at least once a week in cool weather but more often when it's warm. Sugar solutions spoil easily, and harmful bacteria or mold could seriously harm the birds.

Where should I put the hummingbird feeder?

Place your feeder where the birds can easily see it. You can move it closer to your window once they arrive. The feeder should be within 15 feet (4.57 m) of shelter for the birds, near trees and bushes if possible, and not in full sun. Hang the feeder with wire or twine from a tree limb or other support. You can also hang red ribbons near the feeder to get the birds' attention sooner. If the males at your feeder are aggressive, provide another feeder so that they won't have to share just one.

When should I feed hummingbirds?

If you live in the northern United States or Canada, begin putting food out in the spring. Leave your feeders up for two to three weeks after you see the last hummingbird in the fall to provide food for more northern birds on their way south. If you live in the Southwest, you can feed the birds that winter over in your area for 12 months of the year.

What should I feed hummingbirds?

You can buy nectar mixtures, but it's almost silly to do so since it's so easy to make. Just combine 1 part sugar with 4 parts water in a saucepan and boil for one to two minutes. Cool and fill your feeder. Store any extra solution in the refrigerator. Never add red food coloring, since it can harm the birds.

Don't use honey or artificial sweeteners. Honey spoils quickly and can become poisonous, and artificial sweeteners have no nutritional value. If the temperature is very warm, provide a new solution every 48 hours so that it won't spoil.

Hummingbirds also must have plenty of protein in the form of insects and spiders. Put out old bananas somewhere near your nectar feeder. Bananas will draw fruit flies, which hummers love!

Should I provide water for the hummingbirds?

You can provide bathing water for them with a mister hooked up to a garden hose. You'll have great fun watching the tiny birds zoom through the spray! Providing a pan with very shallow water for drinking is a good idea, too.

What should I do about the insects that also use my feeder?

Your feeder may attract ants, bees, and wasps, and they are not especially welcome. The stinging insects may make it difficult for you to get your feeder to clean it. Here are some suggestions that may help.

To deal with ants, put petroleum jelly on the pole or wire holding the feeder. If ants are a real problem, you can buy a feeder that has a little moat of water around the hanging wire of the feeder so that the ants can't cross.

To keep bees and wasps away, look for a feeder with a "bee guard," which is like a screened cage that fits over the feeder holes so that bees can't get close enough to drink. You can also put petroleum jelly, salad oil, or mineral oil around the nectar holes so that the insects can't alight there. Be careful to apply it only at the nectar holes, not in the opening.

If these methods don't work, spray the feeder with your hose when you want to remove it to clean it. The bees or wasps will fly away quickly!

Hummingbird Activities

Plant a Hummingbird Garden

ACTIVITY 1

When you make a garden for hummingbirds, you will also enjoy the beauty of the flowers and other lovely visitors like butterflies. While hummingbirds will try to feed at any flower with nectar, certain flowers are especially adapted (designed for survival) to hummers. The flower's pollen is carried from plant to plant by the birds, ensuring the plant's survival. Most of these flowers are red.

Bees cannot detect the color red, and the flowers have no fragrance, so the bees are not especially attracted to them. Most of these flowers have nectar at the end of long tubular flowers. Hummingbirds can reach this nectar, but bees and other pollinators can't.

When choosing plants for hummers, you can consider both wildflowers and seeds and plants that you buy in garden centers or from seed catalogs. If you don't have room for a garden, a flower box or a few outdoor containers will do nicely.

You can plant several types of flowers:

Annuals live only one year and must be replaced each year. They bloom for a long time and are great for containers.

Biennials live for two years but bloom only in their second year.

Perennials bloom for years and are great for larger gardens.

Whichever plants you choose, don't use chemical pesticides!

Here's a basic list of flowers that attract hummingbirds, but do some research to find more. There are so many possibilities! Ask your parents to bring this list with them to a local garden center and find ones that are suitable for your area. You can also buy seed mixtures collected just for hummers.

Hummingbird garden favorites: trumpet creeper and cardinal flower

Perennial Flowers	Annual Flowers
Bee balm (monarda)	Beardtongue
Cardinal flower	Fire spike
Columbine	Fuchsia
Coralbells	Impatiens
Four-o'clock	Jacobiana
Hollyhock	Jewelweed
Hosta	Painted lady runner beans
Little cigar	Petunia
Lupine	Red salvia
Penstemon	Scarlet sage
Yucca	Shrimp plant

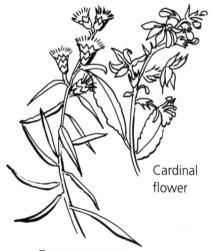

Cardinal flower

Trumpet creeper

Vines	Trees and Shrubs
Cypress vine	Azalea
Honeysuckle	Butterfly bush
Japanese honey-	Flowering
suckle	quince
Morning glory	Lantana
Trumpet creeper	Manzanita
	Mimosa
	Red buckeye
	Turk's cap
	Weigela

A great web site for hummingbird gardening is
www.texasbirdwatcher.com. This comprehensive site explains
how and where to plant each flower species.

ACTIVITY 2

Make Your Own Hummingbird Feeder

It's easy to buy a hummingbird feeder,
but more fun to make one. Remember, the
more feeders you provide, the less likely it
is that the feisty hummers will fight over
the nectar!

Procedure:

1. Use a large nail to make a hole in
   the bottle about 2 inches (5.08
   cm) from the cap. Ask an adult to
   help with this. The hole should be
   big enough to fit the straw
   through.

2. Push the straw into the hole, almost to the
   cap. Adjust it so that the "nectar"—a sugar-
   water solution—won't spill out.

3. Glue the straw where it meets the hole in the
   bottle.

Hummingbird
feeder

> **You will need:**
>
> a small plastic soda
>   bottle
>
> a large nail
>
> a drinking straw
>
> waterproof glue
>
> rope or heavy twine
>
> red ribbons or red paper
>   chains
>
> adult help

4. Tie the rope or twine around the bottom of the bottle so that you can hang it upside down.

5. Make five or six red paper chain links or use red ribbons to attract the hummers. Tie the chains or ribbons from the rope or twine. Don't use too many, or they might be frightened, if indeed hummers are ever frightened by anything!

6. Fill the bottle with the nectar mix and hang it from a pole or tree branch.

Be patient. It may take a while for the birds to discover your feeder.

ACTIVITY
3

Keep a Hummingbird Journal

A journal about your hummingbird visitors might include information, art, and creative writing. Here are some ideas to get you started.

Hummingbird Observations:

◆ When did you see the first hummingbird at your feeder or in the garden?

◆ When did you see the last one in the late summer or fall?

◆ Were the male hummers aggressive? If so, were they aggressive toward one another or toward other creatures such as birds, bees, or dragonflies?

◆ Are males or females or both coming to your hummingbird feeder? Find out how to identify an **immature** or young hummer. (*Clue:* Look for the amount of color on the bird's **gorget,** the colorful neck area on the bird. No color on the gorget means the bird is immature or female. The immatures get more color gradually if they're males.)

◆ Which flowers do the birds visit most often?

- Have you seen the sphinx moth, which looks so much like a hummer? It's also called the hummingbird moth and may come to your feeder.

- Try to find where the hummers are bathing. It's fun to discover them splashing in water on a big leaf.

Creative Fun

Write a poem or story in your journal about hummingbirds. Think about how they capture your imagination. Why are they so interesting? Your poem or story might combine fact with fiction. To get poem or story ideas, think about the amazing hummingbird migration, the bird's feisty behavior, or its iridescent beauty.

Hummer Art

If you like to draw, sketch the hummers where you see them: perched on a branch, hovering at a flower or your feeder, splashing through your sprinkler. You might take photos, too, if you have a lens that can capture such a tiny subject.

9 Butterfly Gardening

As we learned in Chapter 5, brightly colored butterflies are both lovely and interesting insects. We found out about the butterfly's dramatic life cycle of metamorphosis from egg to larva (caterpillar) to adult. While most butterflies live only 10 to 20 days, they need a place to lay eggs, food plants for the larva (called host plants), a place to make a chrysalis, and nectar sources for the adult. Your backyard can provide all or some of what they need for survival in their various life stages. Butterfly gardening is a great way to do just that! You will also be helping with butterfly conservation. Owing to so much human development, there have been great losses of butterfly habitats, and therefore butterfly species.

Butterflies

Planting a large butterfly garden might require lots of adult help, but you can easily make a small garden. All you need is a plot of land in a sunny place, a few garden tools, and the plants that butterflies like. This chapter is only meant to give you an introduction to gardening, but you can surely make your garden as lush and lovely as you'd like!

Where should I put the butterfly garden?

Find out what kinds of butterflies live near you and what kinds of plants they use for food. (I offer some suggestions.) If your family already has a garden, you can add some new plants that will attract butterflies. If you are choosing a new spot, be sure it is in an area that gets sun for most of the day, since both butterflies and the plants they like *love* sun.

How do I prepare the garden area?

Once you know where you want your garden and what you want to plant, you will need to prepare the soil. This includes tasks such as removing grass and weeds and loosening the soil with a garden fork or spade. You (or your parents) may need to add fertilizer or **peat moss** if the soil is poor. Each plant has different planting requirements, so you will need help from an adult with this.

If you are purchasing seeds rather than plants, there are directions on the package. Often seeds can be started inside in small pots in the early spring and then planted in the garden when they are hardy enough. There are many wildflower (perennial) mixes to choose from as well as annuals.

What kind of flowers should I plant?

You want to choose both nectar plants for the adult butterflies to drink from and host plants where the butterflies can lay eggs and on which the larva can feed. Most caterpillars are very fussy eaters and will eat only plants meant for their development.

Butterflies like plants that have pink, red, purple, yellow, or orange flowers. They seem most attracted to large areas of one color or related colors rather than mixed colors. If you have little planting room, choose the butterfly bush, which attracts a wide variety of species.

Remember, you will have to do some research to find out which butterflies live in your area.

Here are some examples of butterfly species (both adult and larva) and the plants they like best:

Butterfly Species	Larval Food	Nectar
Monarch	Milkweed	Milkweed
		Butterfly bush
		Goldenrod
		Thistle
		Mints
Comma	Nettle	Rotting fruit and sap
	Elm	Butterfly bush
		Dandelion
Painted lady	Daisy	Goldenrod
	Hollyhock	Aster
		Zinnia
		Butterfly bush
		Milkweed
Great swallowtail	Citrus trees	Lantana
	Prickly ash	Japanese honeysuckle
		Milkweed
		Lilac
		Goldenrod
		Azalea
Red admiral	Nettle	Rotting fruit and sap
		Daisy
		Aster
		Goldenrod
		Butterfly bush
		Milkweed
Tiger swallowtail	Cherry	Butterfly bush
	Ash	Milkweed
	Birch	Japanese honeysuckle
	Tulip tree	Phlox
	Lilac	Lilac
		Ironweed

Viceroy	Willow	Rotting fruit and sap
	Poplar	Aster
	Apple	Goldenrod
		Milkweed
Buckeye	Snapdragon	Aster
		Milkweed
		Chicory
		Coreopsis
Great spangled fritillary	Violet	Ironweed
		Milkweed
		Black-eyed susan
		Verbena

Other plant and tree suggestions include:

Tithonia
Purple coneflower
Willow, birch, cherry, and poplar trees
Day lily
Joe pye weed
Loosestrife
Clovers
Dill, carrot, parsley
Tulip tree
Mustard family
Lobelia
Lavender
Spicebush
Paw paw
Marigold
Queen Anne's lace

There are many more possibilities, but remember to check with a garden expert to find out which trees, plants, and shrubs do best in your area. Also, note how many species need milkweed. If you don't want to put this plant in your garden, find a separate spot for it. You won't be sorry since it attracts one of the most beautiful butterflies of all . . . the monarch.

Once again, don't use pesticides or even organic pest control products, since they have been found to be harmful to butterflies.

Be patient while you wait for your garden to grow, and more patient still for the butterflies to discover it. Their beautiful arrival will be worth your wait.

Butterfly Activities

Make a Butterfly Feeder

ACTIVITY 1

Can't have a garden? Make this feeder and watch the butterflies come!

You will need:

a small baby food–size jar (or slightly larger)

cotton

sugar solution

a drill (for adult use only)

brightly colored fabric strips

glue

twine

Procedure:

1. Have an adult drill a small hole in the top of the jar.
2. Make sugar solution: Boil one part sugar to nine parts water (no coloring or honey).
3. Plug cotton inside the hole.
4. Fill the bottle with the sugar solution. The cotton will absorb the solution, and the butterfly will "sip" on the cotton.
5. Glue fabric strips to the lid to attract the butterflies.
6. Coil twine around the lid securely, knot, and hang from a branch or pole.

This works best in areas that butterflies frequent.

Make a Butterfly Kite

ACTIVITY 2

You will need:

a butterfly and moth guidebook with color photos or pictures

2 pieces of lightweight paper (8-by-11-inches)

various colors of tissue paper (optional)

scissors

glue

markers

crayons

2 plastic straws

string

You may think that butterfly and moth wings look very fragile, but they are really very strong. A network of veins supports the wings somewhat like the rods of a kite. The veins stiffen the wing and keep it in the right position for flying. You can make your own butterfly or moth kite and decorate its colorful wings.

Procedure:

1. Enlarge and draw the outline and wing patterns of the butterfly you want pictured on your kite. Use a

guidebook to find a colorful wing pattern, or make a bright and interesting pattern of an imaginary butterfly or moth. The wings can be about 6 inches (15 cm) wide on the page.

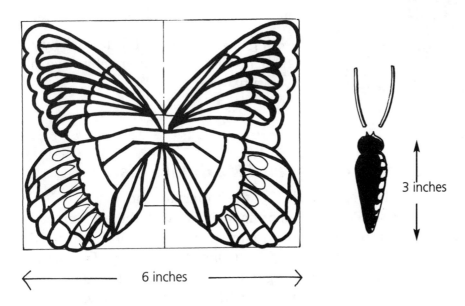

3 inches

6 inches

2. On the other piece of paper, make the butterfly or moth body (as shown) about 3 inches (8 cm) long.
3. Cut antennae 2 inches (5 cm) long from the string.
4. Cut out the wings and the body. Glue the body to the middle of the wings, and glue the antennae onto the head of the butterfly or moth.

5. Lay a 20-foot (6-m) piece of string loosely across the wings. Place the two straws over the string so that they form an X. Then tape them down at their tips.
6. Tie the string tightly around the straws.

Now go fly your kite. While it won't fly very high, it will merrily flutter behind you as you run!

Keep a Butterfly and Moth Life List

Many people keep a "life list" of the butterflies and moths they see. Many often bring their lists with them when they travel so that they can find as many species as possible. You can do this easily, too, by knowing where to look for a variety of moths and butterflies. Look for them in gardens, parks, backyards, and just about anywhere that has flowers with the nectar they love. Look especially near colorful flowers that attract many species. We've provided a basic list, but you can add to it, especially if you live in an area, such as the tropics, where the butterfly and moth species may be different.

You will need:

a butterfly and
   moth guidebook
a hand lens
a sketchbook
colored pencils

Procedure:

1. When you see a butterfly in flight, note its colors and wing patterns. Some species have subtle differences, so observe as carefully as possible. If the butterfly is resting, approach it quietly, and use your hand lens to get a good look at its wing details. The intricate patterns will amaze you!
2. Don't try to pick up butterflies and moths. Their wings are strong, but not strong enough for handling. If you find a really quiet one, you might even get a chance to sketch it. Quickly note the colors and patterns before it flies away.
3. Write down the species on your life list in your sketchbook, noting when and where you saw it. If you find the caterpillar larva of a species, note that also.

Glossary

abdomen   The rear section of the body, which contains the organs of digestion and *reproduction.*

adaptation   Any characteristic that helps a living thing survive in its environment. For example, if the climate in an area changes dramatically, a creature has to make bodily and behavioral changes in order to adapt to those changes and survive.

aerate   To allow air into something.

amphibian   A cold-blooded animal that hatches in the water as *larva* with *gills* and then changes to a lung-breathing adult that dwells at least part of the time on land.

anatomy   A creature's inside and outside body parts.

annelid   A worm with a body made of joined segments or rings.

antenna   A long, thin, movable sense organ on the head of insects and other creatures for smelling and touching. Creatures have two antennae.

anus   The opening at the end of the digestive system where waste is eliminated.

arthropod   Animals without backbones that have joined legs and *segmented* bodies covered by an *exoskeleton.*

biodiversity   The interdependency of the environmental networks that bind together all living creatures, including humans.

biology   The study of living things.

bioluminescence   The chemical reaction that provides certain living things with the ability to produce light.

Bufonidae   The classification given to the family of true toads.

camouflage   The shape or color of an animal that allows it to blend in with its surroundings in order to hide from its predators or to obtain food.

carnivore   An animal that feeds entirely on other animals.

castings   The waste products of the earthworm's digestion.

chrysalis   A capsule enclosing a *pupa* as it transforms from *larva* to adult (for instance, caterpillar to butterfly).

circular muscles   The muscles that *contract* or squeeze together, making the worm's body long and thin. When the *longitudinal* and circular muscles work together, the worm moves.

classes   One of the categories into which all animals are divided. *Phyla* are divided into classes, which are further divided into *orders*.

clitellum   The band or ring around the earthworm's body that produces the mucus needed for fertilization, that is, when the egg of the female joins with the sperm of the male to produce offspring. However, each worm can produce both egg and sperm.

cocoon   The case, often made of silk, of a moth *larva* where the *pupal* stage in its life cycle takes place.

cold-blooded   Having a body temperature that varies with the temperature of the surroundings.

communication   How animals send messages to each other.

compound eyes   The eyes of insects and some other creatures (such as the horseshoe crab). They have many sides and surfaces within their visual makeup.

conclusion   Evaluating the results of an experiment, one tries to reach a conclusion or final judgment about it.

contracting   Squeezing together.

courtship   The process of attracting a mate; in the case of wildlife, courtship often takes place before breeding. Humans demonstrate courtship behaviors, too!

entomologist   A scientist who studies insects.

epiphragm   The dried slime covering the opening to a snail's shell when the creature is cold or dry.

exoskeleton   The outer covering (skin, shell) of an *arthropod* that supports its body like a skeleton.

families   One of the categories into which all animals are divided. *Orders* are divided into families, which are further divided into *genera.*

field marks   In bird-watching, the details of a bird's appearance.

file   A hardened ridge under the cricket's wing that produces sound as it rubs on the wing's *scraper.*

frass   Caterpillar droppings consisting of small brown bits of digested leaves or plant matter.

gastropod   A class in the phylum *mollusks* that includes snails and slugs.

genera   One of the categories into which all animals are divided. *Families* are divided into genera. Each genus is made up of different *species.*

gills   Organs that take air from water so that a creature can breathe.

gizzard   A muscular chamber in the stomach of some creatures that can grind up tough seeds and husks.

gorget   The colorful neck area on a bird.

Gryllidae   The insect family to which crickets belong.

hermaphrodite   Having the characteristics of both a male and a female; each individual produces both egg and sperm and can have babies.

host plant   The plant on which the caterpillar *larva* feeds.

hypothesis   An educated guess or theory about why the results of an investigation occur.

immature   The young of a species that has not yet developed into the adult form.

invertebrate   An animal without a backbone.

Lampyridae   The family to which the firefly belongs.

larva   The *immature* and second stage of *metamorphosis.* For example, the caterpillar is the second stage in the development of the moth or butterfly.

Lepidoptera   The order of insects, including butterflies and moths, that have four wings covered with small scales.

lepidopterist   Someone who studies butterflies and moths.

locomotion   How an animal moves.

longitudinal muscles   The muscles that run lengthwise along a worm's body and draw its body up by squeezing it together. The longitudinal muscles work with the *circular muscles* to help the worm to move.

luciferase   An enzyme (type of protein) that sets off the chemical *luciferin,* which produces the firefly's light.

luciferin   A chemical compound that reacts with oxygen to make the firefly's light.

metamorphosis   The four-stage process of growth and change in a creature's development that involves body changes. Complete meta-morphosis includes egg, *larva, pupal,* and adult stages.

mollusk   An animal, such as a snail, octopus, squid, or scallop, with no backbone and a soft body that is at least partially enclosed by a shell.

molting   The process of shedding an old *exoskeleton* for a new, larger skin that has formed underneath. The new creature that emerges is larger.

nocturnal   Active primarily at night, especially in hunting for food.

nymph   An *immature* or young wingless insect.

ocelli   The simple eyes of insects that can tell the difference between light and dark but cannot see images.

operculum   The hard, flat plate that a snail can use to close the opening to its shell.

orders   One of the categories into which all animals are divided. *Classes* are divided into orders, which are further divided into *families.*

ovipositor   An egg-laying tube in the *abdomen* of the female insect.

peat moss   Moss that grows in very wet places and is often used as a mulch (protective covering) or a plant food.

photocytes   The light cells in the firefly's *abdomen.*

phyla   One of the 26 groups into which all animals are divided. Each phylum is further divided into *classes.*

prediction   A guess about the outcome of an experiment, based on the hypothesis.

pupal stage   The third stage in the *metamorphosis* of an insect in which the *larva* changes into the adult form.

radula   The mouth part of a snail or slug that works like a toothed file; the creature scrapes the radula on a plant and swallows the shredded part.

regenerate   To grow a new part to replace one that has been lost or damaged.

reproduction   The process that allows living things to make more of themselves by breeding and having offspring (young).

scraper   The rough surface of a cricket's wing that rubs against the *file* of the other wing and produces sound.

segmented   Being made up of many small parts.

setae   The bristles, or tiny spines, on each segment of an earthworm that help it to crawl and hold onto surfaces.

slime   A substance secreted by a gland in the foot of a snail or slug that protects it from rough surfaces and helps it to move.

species   A biological classification in which individual creatures are very much alike and can breed and produce offspring.

spiracles   Breathing holes in the body of some animals and insects such as snails, slugs, sharks, rays, and butterflies.

tentacle   A slender, flexible feeler that allows an animal with no backbone to touch things and therefore to find its way.

thorax   The middle section of an insect where the wings or legs are attached.

trials   The repeats of an investigation. The more trials one performs in an experiment, the more reliable or true the results.

tympanal organs   The tight membrane covering the ear of a cricket, which is a tiny hole located under the knees of the cricket's front legs.

vertebrate   An animal with a backbone.

Suggested Reading

Books

Arnold, Caroline. *Fireflies*. New York: Scholastic, 1994.

Bailey, Jill. *How Caterpillars Turn into Butterflies*. New York: Benchmark Books/Marshall Cavendish, 1999.

Berger, Melvin. *Chirping Crickets*. New York: HarperCollins, 1998.

Boring, Mel. *Birds, Nests, and Eggs*. Milwaukee: Gareth Stevens Publishing, 1998.

Brorstrom, Gay Bishop. *A Class Trip to Miss Hallberg's Butterfly Garden*. Sebastpol, Calif: Pipevine Press, 2000.

*Burton, Maurice. *The World of Reptiles and Amphibians*. New York/London: Crown/Bounty Books, 1973.

Cain, Nancy Woodard. *Animal Behavior Science Projects*. New York: John Wiley & Sons, 1998.

*Duensing, Edward. *Talking to Fireflies, Shrinking the Moon*. Golden, Colo: Fulcrum, 1997.

Feltwell, John. *Butterflies and Moths*. New York: Dorling Kindersley, 1993.

Hand, Julia. *The Wonderful World of Wigglers*. Montpelier, Vt.: Food Works, 1995.

* Adult-level reading.

Herberman, Ethan. *The Great Butterfly Hunt.* New York: Simon & Schuster, 1990.

Hogner, Dorothy Childs. *Earthworms.* New York: Thomas Y. Crowell Co., 1953.

Hutchins, Ross E. *Grasshopper and Their Kin.* New York: Dodd, Mead & Co., 1972.

Johnson, Sylvia A. *Chirping Insects.* Minneapolis: Learner Publishing Co., 1986.

———. *Fireflies.* Minneapolis: Learner Publication Co., 1986.

Julivert, Maria Angels. *The Fascinating World of Birds.* New York: Barron's, 1991.

*Kneidel, Sally. *Creepy Crawlies and the Scientific Method.* Golden, Colo.: Fulcrum, 1993.

———. *More Pet Bugs.* New York: John Wiley & Sons, 1999.

———. *Pet Bugs.* New York: John Wiley & Sons, 1994.

———. *Slugs, Bugs, and Salamanders.* Golden, Colo.: Fulcrum, 1997.

Kohn, Bernice. *Fireflies.* Englewood Cliffs, N.J.: Prentice-Hall, 1966.

Koontz, Robin Michal. *The Complete Backyard Nature Activity Book.* New York: Learning Triangle Press/McGraw-Hill, 1998.

*Kramer, David C. *Animals in the Classroom.* Menlo Park, Calif.: Addison-Wesley Longman, 1989.

Latimer, Jonathan, and Karen Nolting. *Peterson Field Guides for Young Naturalists: Caterpillars.* Boston: Houghton Mifflin, 2000.

Lauber, Patricia. *Earthworms: Underground Farmers.* New York: Henry Holt & Co., 1994.

*Lingelbach, Jenepher, ed. *Hands on Nature: Information and Activities for Exploring the Environment with Children.* Woodstock, Vt: Vermont Institute of Natural Science, 1986.

McKeever, Susan. *Butterflies of North America.* San Diego: Thunder Bay Press, 1995.

McLaughlin, Molly. *Earthworms, Dirt, and Rotten Leaves.* New York: Avon/Camelot, 1986.

*Needham, Bobbe. *Beastly Abodes.* New York: Sterling Publishing Co., 1995.

Pascoe, Elaine. *Nature Close-up: Tadpoles.* Woodbridge, Conn.: Blackbirch Press, 1997.

———. *Crickets and Grasshoppers.* Woodbridge, CT: Blackbirch Press, 1999.

Poole, Lynn, and Greg Poole. *Fireflies in Nature and the Laboratory.* New York: Thomas Y. Crowell Co., 1965.

Porter, George. *The World of the Frog and the Toad.* Philadelphia: J. B. Lippincott Co., 1967.

Ross, Michael Elsohn. *Cricketology.* Minneapolis: Carolrhoda Books, 1996.

Schneck, Marcus. *Creating a Butterfly Garden.* New York: Simon & Schuster, 1999.

Simon, Seymour. *Pets in a Jar.* New York: Viking Press, 1975.

VanCleave, Janice. *Biology for Every Kid.* New York: John Wiley & Sons, 1990.

———. *Insects and Spiders.* New York: John Wiley & Sons, Inc., 1998.

Weber, William J. *Attracting Birds and Other Wildlife to Your Yard.* New York: Holt, Rinehart and Winston, 1982.

Webster, David. *Frog and Toad Watching.* New York: Simon & Schuster, 1986.

Internet Sites

www.alienexplorer.com

www.birding.about.com

www.alawildrehab.org

www.enchantedlearning.com

www.learner.org

ericir.syr.edu/Virtual/Lessons/Science/Biological/BIO116.html

www.nwf.org/habitats/backyard

www.uky.edu/Agriculture/Entomology/entfacts/misc/ef006.htm

hgic.clemson.edu/factsheets/HGIC1701.htm

butterflybutterfly.com/Butterflygarden.html

home.jtan.com/~jack/feed/html

Index